The Gentleman of Venice by James Shirley

A TRAGI-COMEDIE. Presented at the Private house in Salisbury Court by her Majesties Servants.

James Shirley was born in London in September 1596.

His education was through a collection of England's finest establishments: Merchant Taylors' School, London, St John's College, Oxford, and St Catharine's College, Cambridge, where he took his B.A. degree in approximately 1618.

He first published in 1618, a poem entitled Echo, or the Unfortunate Lovers.

As with many artists of this period full details of his life and career are not recorded. Sources say that after graduating he became "a minister of God's word in or near St Albans." A conversion to the Catholic faith enabled him to become master of St Albans School from 1623–25.

He wrote his first play, Love Tricks, or the School of Complement, which was licensed on February 10th, 1625. From the given date it would seem he wrote this whilst at St Albans but, after its production, he moved to London and to live in Gray's Inn.

For the next two decades, he would write prolifically and with great quality, across a spectrum of thirty plays; through tragedies and comedies to tragicomedies as well as several books of poetry. Unfortunately, his talents were left to wither when Parliament passed the Puritan edict in 1642, forbidding all stage plays and closing the theatres.

Most of his early plays were performed by Queen Henrietta's Men, the acting company for which Shirley was engaged as house dramatist.

Shirley's sympathies lay with the King in battles with Parliament and he received marks of special favor from the Queen.

He made a bitter attack on William Prynne, who had attacked the stage in Histriomastix, and, when in 1634 a special masque was presented at Whitehall by the gentlemen of the Inns of Court as a practical reply to Prynne, Shirley wrote the text—The Triumph of Peace.

Shirley spent the years 1636 to 1640 in Ireland, under the patronage of the Earl of Kildare. Several of his plays were produced by his friend John Ogilby in Dublin in the first ever constructed Irish theatre; The Werburgh Street Theatre. During his years in Dublin he wrote The Doubtful Heir, The Royal Master, The Constant Maid, and St. Patrick for Ireland.

In his absence from London, Queen Henrietta's Men sold off a dozen of his plays to the stationers, who naturally, enough published them. When Shirley returned to London in 1640, he finished with the Queen Henrietta's company and his final plays in London were acted by the King's Men.

On the outbreak of the English Civil War Shirley served with the Earl of Newcastle. However when the King's fortunes began to decline he returned to London. There his friend Thomas Stanley gave him help and thereafter Shirley supported himself in the main by teaching and publishing some educational works under the Commonwealth. In addition to these he published during the period of dramatic eclipse four small volumes of poems and plays, in 1646, 1653, 1655, and 1659.

It is said that he was "a drudge" for John Ogilby in his translations of Homer's Iliad and the Odyssey, and survived into the reign of Charles II, but, though some of his comedies were revived, his days as a playwright were over.

His death, at age seventy, along with that of his wife, in 1666, is described as one of fright and exposure due to the Great Fire of London which had raged through parts of London from September 2nd to the 5th.

He was buried at St Giles in the Fields on October 29th, 1666.

Index of Contents

SIR,

The Poem that approacheth to kiss your hand, had once a singular grace and lustre from the Scene, when it enjoy'd the life of action; Nor did it want the best hands to applaud it in the Theater; But nothing of these is considerable, to the Honour it may receive now from your Confirmation and acceptance.

I must acknowledge many years have past, since it did Vagire in Cunis, and when it had gotten strength, and legs to walk, traveling without direction, it lost it self, till it was recovered after much inquisition, and now upon the first return home, hath made this fortunate addresse, and application to your Patronage; In which my ambition is satisfied.

I know this Nation hath been fruitfull in names of Eminent Honor. But in these times, there be more Lords then Noblemen, and while you are pleas'd to smile upon this piece, I most cheerfully throw my selfe, and it upon your Protection, whose single worth to me, is beyond all the boasted Greatnesse and voluminous titles of our age.

Be pleas'd to read, what is presented you, at an hour, you will dedicate to Recreation, and preserve the Author in your memory, whose highest desires are to make good the Character of

Sir,
The most humble among,
those that honor you

DRAMATIS PERSONAE

The Duke of Venice.

Cornari a Gentleman of Venice of a great fortune, but having no Child, contrives to have an heir from his wife, and against the nature and custome of the Italian, indeeres an English gentleman to her affection and society.

Florelli the English Gentleman of a Noble extraction and person, much honoured for his parts, by which he gained much reputation in the Academies.

Malipiero Nephew to Cornari, a man of a violent spirit, and hated by his uncle, for his debaucheries.

Giovanni, (suppos'd Son of Roberto the Dukes Gardiner) whose noble mind could not be supprest, in his low condition, and in love with Bellaura.

Thomazo, the supposed Son of the Duke, whom no precepts, nor education at Court, could form into honorable desires, or employments.

Courtiers of Honor.

Marino

Candiano

Roberto the Dukes Gardiner, an humorous jolly old man.

Companions of Malipiero
Bernardo
Marcello
Georgio, the Gardiners servant.
Bravos.
Attendants.
Souldiers.
Bellaura the Dukes Niece, whom Giovanni passionately affected.
Claudiana wife to Gornari, a Lady of excellent beauty, ingratiated by her husband to Florelli the english Gentleman.
Ursula wife to Roberto, a froward woman, and who much doted upon Thomazo her Nursechild.
Rosabella a Curtesan.

SCENE - VENICE

THE GENTLEMAN OF VENICE

ACT I

SCENE I

A Street Before Cornari's House.

Enter **MALIPIERO**, who knocks at a Door, to him a **SERVANT**.

MALIPIERO
Where is my Uncle sirra?

SERVANT
Not within.

MALIPIERO
Come hither, tell me truth.

SERVANT
He's gone abroad.

MALIPIERO
He has commanded your officious rogueship.
To deny him to me.

[**MALIPIERO** kicks him.

SERVANT
What do you mean sir?

MALIPIERO
To speak with my Uncle sirrah, and these kicks
Shall fetch him hither.

SERVANT
Help.

[He runs in.

MALIPIERO
Your howling will
Be his kue to appear.

[Enter **CORNARI**.

CORNARI
What insolence is this?

MALIPIERO
No insolence: I did but correct your knave,
Because I would not lose my labour sir,
I came to speak w'ee.

CORNARI
Shall I not be safe
Within my house? hence.

MALIPIERO
I ha not done yet.

CORNARI
You were best assault me too.

MALIPIERO
I must borrow money,
And that some call a striking; but you are
My very loving Uncle, and do know
How necessary it is, your Nephew should not
Want for your honor.

CORNARI
Hence; I disclaim,
And throw thee from my blood; thou art a bastard.

MALIPIERO

Indeed you do lie Uncle, and 'tis love,
And reverence bids me say so, it would cost
Dear, should the proudest Gentleman of Venice
Have call'd my Mother whore, but you shall onely
By the disbourse of fifty Duccats take
My anger off, and I'le be still your Nephew,
And drink your health, and my good Aunts.

CORNARI

Drink thy
Confusion.

MALIPIERO

Heaven forbid your Heir should so
Forget himself, and lose the benefit
Of such a fair Estate as you have Uncle;
Shall I have Gold for present use?

CORNARI

Not a Zechine.

MALIPIERO

Consider but what Company I keep.

CORNARI

Things that lie like Consumptions on their Family,
And will in time eat up their very name;
A knot of fooles and knaves.

MALIPIERO

Take heed, be temperate,
A hundred Duccats else wil hadly satisfie,
The Dukes own Son Signior Thomazo wo'not
Blush to be drunk sir in my company.

CORNARI

He is corrupted
Amongst diseases like thy self, become
His Fathers shame and sorrow, and hath no
Inheritance of his noble nature.

MALIPIERO

You
Were best call him bastard too, the money
I modestly demanded, and that quickly,
And quietly, before I talk aloud,
I may be heard to'th Palace else.

CORNARI
Thou heard? i'le tel thee,
Were treason talk'd, I believe thy testimony
Would hold no credit against the hangman, but
I lose too pretious time in dialogue with thee,
To be short therefore know.—

MALIPIERO
Very well, to'th point.

CORNARI
I will consume all my estate my self.

MALIPIERO
You do not know the waies without instruction.

CORNARI
I will be instructed then.

MALIPIERO
I doe like that,
Let's join societies, and ile be satisfied;
Let me have part in the consuming of
The money, that does mould for want of Sun-beams
Within your musty Coffers, I'le release you.
You have no swaggering face; but I can teach
Your very lookes to make a noyse, and if
You cannot drink or game, wee'l ha' devices;
You may have whores, I that but live in hope
After your death, keep twelve in pension,
They wear my Livery, I'le resigne the Leverets,
I can ha more, I have a list of all
The Curtezans in Venice, which shall tumble
And keep their bugle bowes for thee dear Uncle,
Wee'l teach thee a thousand waies.

CORNARI
It shannot need,
I shall take other courses with my wealth,
And none of you shall share in't. I have a humour
To turn my money into Hospitalls;
Your riots come not thither.

MALIPIERO
But we may,
Drink, and diseases are the waies to that too,
But will you turn a Master of this Colledge

You talk of Uncle? this same Hospitall?
And lay out money to buy wooden leggs
For crippl'd men of War, invite to your cost
Men that have lost their noses in hot service?
Live and converse with roten bawdes & bonesetters,
Provide Pensions for surgery, and hard words
That eat like Corrosives, and more afflict
The patient? but you'll save charges, I consider
My Aunt, your wife—

CORNARI
How darst thou mention her
With thy foul breath.

MALIPIERO
May be excellent at composing
Of Med'cines for corrupted lungs, impostumes
At making plaisters, dyet drinks, and in charity
Will be a great friend to the pox.

CORNARI
Thou villain.

MALIPIERO
And you'l be famous by'c, I may in time
As I said before, if lust, and wine assist me,
Grow unsound too, and be one of her patients;
And have an office after in her houshold
To prepare lint, and fearcloths, empty veines,
And be controller of the Crutches, oh
The world would praise the new foundation
Of such a Pest house, and the poor soules drink
Your health at every Festivall in hot porredge.

CORNARI
Art thou of kin to me?

MALIPIERO
I think I am,
As near as your brothers eldest Son, who had
No competent estate from his own parents.
And for that reason by wise nature was
Ordain'd to be your heir that have enough Uncle.
The fates must be obeyed, and while your land
Is fastned to my name for want of males,
Which I do hope, if my Aunt hold her barrennesse
You will never bang out of her Sheaf, I may
Be confident to write my self your Nephew.

CORNARI
Thou hast no seeds of goodness in thee, but
I may find waies to cross your hopefull interest.

MALIPIERO
You'l find no seeds in my Aunts parslybed
I hope, and then I'm safe, but take your course,
Supply me for the present, for your honour—
The Duccats come.

CORNARI
You are cosened.

MALIPIERO
As you would not
Have me pull down this house, when you are dead
And build a stewes, the Duccats come.

CORNARI
Thou coward!

MALIPIERO
Because I do not cut your throat, that were
The way to disinherit my self queintly.

CORNARI
Canst thou not steal? & so deserve a hanging?

MALIPIERO
Yes I can, and am often tempted, but I wo'not
Do you that mighty wrong, to let what you have
So long, and with so little conscience gathered,
Be lost in confiscation by my fellony.
I know a way worth ten on't; yet thus much
I'le bind it with an oath, when I turn thief,
Your Gold shall be the first I will make bold with,
In the mean time lend me the trifling Duccats,
And do not trouble me.

CORNARI
Not a Muccinigo
To save thee from the Gallies.

MALIPIERO
No? the Gallies!
Must I shift still? remember, and die shortly
I'le live, I will, and `rather then not be

Reveng'd on thy estate, I will eat roots
Course ones I mean, love, and undoe an herbwife
With eating up her sallets, live and lap
Onely in barly water, think on't yet,
I am now for wine, you know not what that heat
May do, the injury being so fresh, I may
Return, and you'l repent.

CORNARI
'Tis more then I
Can hope of thee, go to your rabble sir.

MALIPIERO
You a Gentleman of Venice? but remember,
A pox 'a your wealth, I will do something
To deserve the halter, that I may disgrace
The house I came on, and at my Execution
Make such a speech, as at the report, thou shalt
Turn desperate, and with the remnant of
My Cord go hang thy self, and that way forfeit
All thy Estate when I am dead, i'le do
Or this, or something worse to be reveng'd.

[Exit **MALIPIERO**

[Enter **SERVANT**.

CORNARI
Hee's lost, this doth new fire my resolution;
See if your Mistris be yet ready sirra,
Say I expect her.

[Exit **SERVANT**.

My blood is almost in a fever with
My passion, but Claudiana may cure all,
Whom I have wrought with importunity
To be spectator at the exercise
This day 'ith Academy, here she comes,

[Enter **CLAUDIANA**.

Art ready?

CLAUDIANA
Ever to obey you sir,
But if you would consider yet, you may
Be kind, and let me stay, I dare not think

You are less careful of my honor, but
You gave once Command with my consent too,
Not to be seen too much abroad.

CORNARI
I did.
I must confesse Claudiana, I had thoughts
And scruples which thy innocence hath clear'd,
And though our nice Italian every where
Impose severely on their wives; I should
Be unjust to make thee still a prisoner to
Thy melancholly Chamber, take the aire,
'Tis for thy health, and while I wait upon thee,
Thou art above the tongue, and wound of scandall.

CLAUDIANA
I know your presence takes off all dishonor,
But—

CORNARI
No more, I charge thee by thy love,
And to convince all arguments against it;
I have provided so, thou shalt observe
Unseen the bold contentions of art,
And action.

CLAUDIANA
I'm not well.

CORNARI
I shall be angry
If my desires be plai'd withall, pretend not
With purpose to delude me, I have blessings
Stor'd in thy health, but if you practise any
Infirmity to cross my will, that aimes
At the security of thy health and honour—

CLAUDIANA
Sir, you shall steere me.

CORNARI
This becomes Claudiana,
I will think thee in a kiss, prepare
The Gundelo.

SERVANT [Within]
It waites

CORNARI
And I on thee,
The treasure of my eyes, and heart.

[Exeunt.

SCENE II

The Duke's Gardens

[Enter **ROBERTO, URSULA, GEORGIO**.

ROBERTO
Where is my son Giovanni sirra?

GEORGIO
He went two hours ago to the Academy,
To see the exercise to day.

URSULA
How's that?
What business has he there, pray 'mongst Gentlemen?
He does presume too much.

ROBERTO
Patience good Ursula.

URSULA
You give him to much reine; 'twould become him
To follow his profession, and not look after
Those gentlemanly sports.

ROBERTO
No tempest wife,
No thundring Ursula, am not I the Dukes
Chief Gardiner, Ha! and shall I make my Son
A drudg; confine him here to be an earth-worm,
Live like a mole, or make it his last blessing
To plant, and order quickset; let him walk,
And see the fashions.

URSULA
He has cost you sweetly
To bring him up, what use had he of learning?
What benefit, but to endanger us,
And with his 'poring upon books at midnight,

To set the house on fire, let him know how
To rule a spade, as you ha done.

ROBERTO
He does so,
And knowes how to inoculate my Ursula,
My nimble tongue, no more: because he read
The story of Zantippe to'ther night
That could out-talk a drum, and sound a point
Of War to her husband honest Socrates,
You took a pet; he shall abroad sometimes
And read and write till his head ake. Go to

URSULA
So, so, the Dukes Garden shall be then
Well look't to, he deserves a Pension,
For reading Amadis de gaule, and Guzman,
And Don Quixot, but i'le read him a lecture.

ROBERTO
You will? offer but to bark at him,
And I will send him to the University
To anger thee, nay he shall learn to fence too,
And fight with thee, at twenty severall weapons
Except thy two edged tongue, a little thing
Would make me entertain a dancing master,
Peace, or I will destroy thy Kitchin Ursula,
Disorder all thy trinkets, and in stead
Of brasse and pewter, hang up Violl de Gambos,
I'le set an Organ up at thy beds head,
And he shall play upon't: what tyrannicall
To thy own flesh and blood, to Giovanni?
My heir, my onely boy? fetch me a taylor,
He shall have new cloaths, and no more be warm
With the reversion of your peticoates,
Do not provoke me, what imperious?
Get you in, or I will swinge you, go, and weed.

URSULA
Now for vexation could I cry my heart out.

[Exit.

ROBERTO
Sirra stay you, and is Giovanni gone
To'th' Academy saist?

GEORGIO

Yes sir, they say,
There is an English Gentleman, that winns
The Garland from 'em all at every exercise,
One of the Court told my young master on't,
(As he enquired of every Gentleman
Comes in to'th' Garden, what's the newes abroad)

ROBERTO
And does he not tell thee tales & dainty stories
Sometimes?

GEORGIO
Oh, of Tamberlain, and the great Turk, & all
His Concubines, he knowes 'em to a hair,
He is more perfect in the Chronicles
Then I am in my prayers.

ROBERTO
I do believ't

GEORGIO
And talkes a battell, as he were among 'em,
He tickles all your turbants, and in a rage,
Wishes he had the cutting of their Cabbages
To shew what house he came on.

ROBERTO
Ha my boy!

GEORGIO
Oh sir he has a pestilent memory,
He told me to'ther day there was another
World in the Moon, and that the world we live in
Shines like to that, to people that live there,
How many miles it is about the Earth,
How many to the starrs, I fear he will
Be mad, if he read much, 'tis just like ravening,
And such hard words would choak me to repeat 'em.

ROBERTO
He never tells me this.

GEORGIO
We are familiar.
You are his Father, and he dares not lie
To you, to me he may talk any thing,
He knowes my understanding to an inch.
Would you would speak to him though, to take a little

More paines, 'tis I do all the droile, the durtwork:
When I am digging; he is cutting Unicornes,
And Lyons in some hedge, or else devising
New knots upon the ground, drawing out Growns
And the Dukes armes, Castles and Cannons in 'em,
Here Gallies, there a Ship giving a broad side,
Here out of turfe he carves a Senatour
With all his robes, making a speech to Time
That grows hard by, and twenty curiosities,
I think he meanes to embroider all the Garden
Shortly, but I do all the course-worke; here's
My Mistris agen.

[Enter **URSULA**.

ROBERTO
What, is the storm laid?

URSULA
I must be patient: your sonne's not come yet

ROBERTO
Why now thou art Vrsa Maior, love thy whelp,
And we are friends.

URSULA
Was not the Dukes Son here?
I fear he is sick, that I have not seen him
These two daies in the Garden.

GEORGIO
There's a Gentleman.

URSULA
I, there's a Gentleman indeed.
I dream't on him last night, pray heaven he be
In health, I prethee make enquiry,
There's a Gentleman, and you talk of a Gentleman.

GEORGIO
Signior Thomazo?

ROBERTO
Where is hee?

GEORGIO
I know not, but my mistris would send me
To know the state of his body.

ROBERTO

Why, how now Ursula? sirra about you businesse,
And spare that inquisition, what hath
Your impudence to do with the Dukes Son?

URSULA

Have not I to do that gave him suck?
I hope I was his nurse, and it becomes me
To enquire of his health, he is the very pearl
Of curtesie, not proud nor coy I warrant you,
But gentle as my Sunday muffe.

ROBERTO

Your conny skinne.

URSULA

I am the better when I look upon him,
There' a gentleman, and you talk of a gentleman,
So compleat, so affable, a scholar too,
If I could understand him, prethee sweet heart,
Get me with child that I may long a little.

ROBERTO

For a piece of the Dukes Son?

URSULA

I shall nere forget how pretily
He took the niple, and would play, and prattle himself
A sleep I warrant you, but hee's now a man,
A great man, and he remembers me still:
There's a gentleman, and you talk of a gentleman.

ROBERTO

The woman dotes.

[Exit.

SCENE III

A Street.

[Enter **MARINO** meeting **CANDIANO** a Senatour.

MARINO

Whither so fast?

CANDIANO
To the Academy.

MARINO
Spare
Your hast, all's done.

CANDIANO
Who has the vote to day?

MARINO
The English Gentleman is still victorious▪
All praises flow upon him, he ha's depos'd
Our City, which hath now resign'd her Lawrell.

[Enter **FLORELLI** and other **GENTLEMEN**.

CANDIANO
Is not this he?

MARINO
The same, in's face the promise
Of a most noble nature.
FLORELLI
Gentlemen,
Pray give me leave, to understand your language,
For this, so much above me, scarce will be,
(When I'm lesse ignorant), worth my thanks,

1ˢᵗ GENTLEMAN
This is
We know pretence of modesty, we must
Congratulate your triumph.

FLORELLI
For this time
I'le be content your praises shall abuse me.
Who are these?

MARINO
Friends and Honorers of your worth.

FLORELLI
I see that courtesie is native here,
All the reward I can return, must be
To speak abroad the Noblenesse of Venice
For so much grace to an unworthy stranger.

CANDIANO
The Duke himselfe.

[Enter **DUKE, THOMAZO, SENATORS, MALIPIERO.**

DUKE
We must resolve to send new forces
And speedily, the flame will else endanger
Venice it self.

SENATOR
This town lost will encourage
The insulting Genowese.

DUKE
Thomazo!

THOMAZO
Sir.

DUKE
I look when you will ask me leave to traile
A pike, and purchase honor in these Warrs.

THOMAZO
I have not been well since I was last
Let blood, and therefore if you please, I would
Be excus'd till the next warrs, and then have at 'em▪
By that time I shall be a better rapier man.

DUKE
This fool is the dishonor of my blood,
He declines all that's noble, and obeyes
A base and vulgar appetite, he dwells
Like a disease within my name, but 'tis
Heavens punishment, what are they?

MALIPIERO
All strangers, but among them one
In whom you may read something worth your grace,
An English Gentleman.

DUKE
He, to whom fame
Gives the honor of our exercises, nature
With such an active heat might have built up
My Son, but hee's curst to live a shadow,

Marino fetches Florelli to kiss the Dukes hand.
Welcome sir to Venice.

THOMAZO
He shall kiss my hand too, I am the Dukes Son.

FLORELLI
You honor me.

DUKE
Thomazo give that gentleman
A box 'oth ear.

THOMAZO
He wo'not take it kindly,
He is one—

DUKE
Will strike agen, is not that it?

THOMAZO
I would not use a stranger so discourteously, or else—

DUKE
Embrace him then, and make your self worthy of
His friendship and converse, you'l gain more honor
Then the empty title of your birth can bring yee:
But to the great affair; the War, your Counsells.

[Exeunt **DUKE**, **SENATOR** and **MARINO**.

THOMAZO
My father bids me embrace you sir.

FLORELLI
I shall
Be proud when I can do you any service.

THOMAZO
Gentlemen, pray know me every one
I am the Dukes Son, my name's Signior Thomazo.

GENTLEMAN
You do us too great honor.

MALIPIERO
We had no object worth our envy sir
Till you arriv'd, you have at once dishonored,

And made our Venice fortunate.

THOMAZO
Malipiero, let's bid 'em welcome in rich wine.

MALIPIERO
I attend you sir.
This fellow must not live to boast his trophees,
He may supplant me too, if he converse
Too freely with Thomazo, whose course wit
Is all the stock I live by, please you gentlemen
To walk.

GENTLEMAN
We follow.

THOMAZO
I would not have the way
But that you are a stranger.

GENTLEMAN
it becomes you.

[Exit **OMNES**.

ACT II

SCENE I

The Duke's Gardens.

Enter **CORNARI** and **CLAUDIANA,** as in the Duke Garden.

CLAUDIANA
II have obey'd you sir.

CORNARI
Thou hast done well
My Claudiana, very well, who dare
Traduce thee for't? am I not carefull of thee?
I prethee give me thy opinion
Who deserv'd best of all the gentlemen?

CLAUDIANA
I have not art enough to judge.

CORNARI
But thou
Hast fancie, and a liberall thought, that may
Bestow thy praise on some or other, tell me
If thou hadst been to give the garland, prethee
Whose head should wear it? though wee ha not judgement
To examine, and prepare our justice; yet
Where men contend for any victory,
Affection may dispose us, and by some
Secret in nature we do still incline
To one, and guard him with our wishes.

CLAUDIANA
I hope
This is but mirth.

CORNARI
By my regard to thy
Fair honor, nothing else, it shannot rise
To a dispute, who ha's the vote to day
Of all the gentlemen? I must know.

CLAUDIANA
They are
To me indifferent.

CORNARI
So is my question, but I must have more,
It cannot be but some man must deserve
More print and poize in thy opinion,
Speak as thou lov'st me Claudiana.

CLAUDIANA
Sir,
Your inquisition is not without change
Of looks upon me, and those smiles you ask with,
Are not your own I fear.

CORNARI
Nay, then you dally,
And undoe that obedience, I so much
Commended.

CLAUDIANA
Dear Cornari.

CORNARI
Yet agen?

The man, tell me the man?

CLAUDIANA
What man?

CORNARI
The gentleman
That best deserves in thy opinion.
I shall be angry: what deny to give me
This triviall satisfaction? the expence
Of a little breath? why do you tremble so?

CLAUDIANA
Alas, I know not what to answer, this
Must needs engender fears in my cold bosome,
That my poor honor is betrai'd, and I
Stand in your thoughts suspected of some guilt
I never understood, if the report
Of malice have abus'd me to your ear,
(For by your self I am all innocent)

CORNARI
What do you mean Claudiana?

CLAUDIANA
Sir, your question
Hath frighted me, 'tis strange, and killing to
My tender apprehension.

CORNARI
Y'are a fool
To be thus troubled, and but that I know
The purity of thy faith to me, this language
Would make me jealous, 'tis an ill dress't passion,
And palenesse, that becomes not Claudiana
To wear upon her modest cheek, I see
Thy heart sick in thy eyes, be wise, and cure it,
My question was but mirth, without the sence
Of the least scruple in my self, or meaning
To discompose one chearfull look.

CLAUDIANA
Your pardon.

CORNARI
And you as safely might have answered me.
As I had casually ask't the time o'th day;
What dressing you delight in, or what gown

You most affect to wear.

CLAUDIANA
Once more I ask you pardon, you restore me,
And I am now secur'd by your clear goodnesse,
To give my weak opinion—

CORNARI
Of the man
That did appear in thy thoughts to deserve
Most honor.

CLAUDIANA
You'l excuse a womans verdict,
My voice is for the stranger sir.

CORNARI
Why so!
You like him best; what horror was in this
Poor question now? you mean the English man?

CLAUDIANA
The same, most gracefull in his parts & person.

CORNARI
'Tis well, I'me satisfied, and we both meet
In one opinion too, he is indeed
The bravest Cavalier, what hurt's in all
This now? I see you can distinguish, wert thou
A virgin Claudiana, thou would'st find
Gentle and easie thoughts to entertain
So promising a servant; I should be
Taken with him my self, were I a Lady,
And lov'd a man.

CLAUDIANA
How's this? my feares return.

[Enter **BELLAURA** and **GEORGIO**.

CORNARI
Madam Bellaura the Dukes charge is entred
The Garden, let's choose another walk.

[Exit.

BELLAURA
Why you are conceited sirra, does wit

Grow in this Garden?

GEORGIO
Yea, Madam while I am in't, I am a slip
My self.

BELLAURA
Of Rosemary or time?

GEORGIO
Of wit sweet Madam.

BELLAURA
'Tis pitty, but thou shouldst be kept with watering,

GEORGIO
There's wit in every Flower, if you can gather it.

BELLAURA
I am of thy mind.
But what's the wit prethee of yonder tulip?

GEORGIO
You may read there the wit of a young Courtier.

BELLAURA
What's that?

GEORGIO
Pride, and shew of colours, a fair promising,
Deare when 'tis bought, and quickly comes to nothing.

BELLAURA
The wit of that rose?

GEORGIO
If you attempt
Madam to pluck a rose, I shall find a moral in't.

BELLAURA
No Country wit?

GEORGIO
That growes with pot-herbes, and poor roots, which here
Would be accounted weeds, course things of profit,
Whose end is kitchin Physick, and sound health;
Two things not now in fashion.

BELLAURA
Your wit dances.
Where learn't you all these moralls?

GEORGIO
I but glean
From my young master Giovanni Madam,
Hee'l run division upon every flower,
He ha's a wit able to kill the weeds,
And ripen all the fruit in the Dukes Orchard.

BELLAURA
Where is Giovanni?

GEORGIO
He went betimes to'th Academy,
He is at all the exercises, we
Shall ha such newes when he comes home.

BELLAURA
Why does
Your master (being rich) suffer his son
To work i'th garden?

GEORGIO
My master? hee's an honest mortall man Madam,
It is my mistriss, that commands him to't,
A shrow, and loves him not, but 'tis no matter;
I ha' the better company, hee's here.

[Enter **GIOVANNI**.

I'le leave him to you Madam, I must now
Water my plants.

[Exit.

BELLAURA
Why? how now Giovanni, you frequent I hear
The Academies.

GIOVANNI
When I can dispence
Madam, with time, and these employments, I
Intrude a glad spectator at those schooles
Of wit and action, which although I cannot
Reach, I am willing to admire, and look at
With pitty of my self lost here in darknesse.

BELLAURA

By this expression I may conceive
How much you have improv'd, & gain'd a language
Courtly, and modest.

GIOVANNI

Madam, you are pleas'd
To make my uneven frame of words your mirth.
I professe nothing but an humble ignorance,
And I repent not, if by any way
(My duty and manners safe) it may delight you.

BELLAURA

Indeed Giovanni I am pleas'd, but not
With your suspition, that my praises are
Other then what become my ingenuous meaning,
For if I understand, I like your language,
But with it I commend your modest spirit.

GIOVANNI

It is an honour Madam, much above
My youths ambition, but if I possesse
A part of any knowledge you have dain'd
To allow, it owes it self unto this school.

BELLAURA

What school?

GIOVANNI

This Garden Madam, 'tis my Academy,
Where gentlemen, and Ladies (as your self,
The first and fairest, durst I call you mistris,)
Enrich my eare, and observation
With harmony of language, which at best
I can but coldly imitate.

BELLAURA

Still more courtly!
Why how now Giovanni, you will be
Professor shortly in the art of complement,
You were best quit the Garden, & turn Courtier.

GIOVANNI

Madam, I think upon the Court with reverence,
My fate, is to adore it afar off,
It is a glorious Landschape, which I look at
As some men with narrow optick glasses

Behold the starrs, and wonder at their vast
(Though unknown) habitable worlds of brightness:
But were my eye a nearer judge, and I
Admitted to a clearer knowledge Madam
Of the Court life, there I might find the truth
Of mans best Ideas, and enjoy the happinesse,
Now onely mine by naked speculation,
I think how there I should throw off my dust
And rise a new Creation.

BELLAURA
The Court
Is much beholding to you Giovanni.

GIOVANNI
It is a duty Madam I owe truth.

BELLAURA
A truth in supposition all this while.

GIOVANNI
I should be sad if any experience should
Betray an error in my faith, and yet
So soft and innocent a trespasse, Madam,
Might well expect a pardon.

BELLAURA
Some that have
Freely enjoy'd the pleasures, or what else
You so advance in Court, have at the last
Been weary, and accus'd their gay Condition,
Nay, chang'd their state for such an humble life
As you professe, a gardiner.

GEORGIO
I despise not
What I was born to Madam, but I should
Imagine the disease lay in the mind,
Not in the Courtier, that would throw away
So spacious a blessing to be servile.

BELLAURA
You know not Giovanni your own happiness,
Nor the Court sinnes, the pride and surfeits there
Come not within your circle, there are few
Pursue those noble tracts your fancy aims at,
It is a dangerous Sea to launch into,
Both shelves and rockes you see not, I, & mermaids.

GIOVANNI
What are they Madam?

BELLAURA
You have heard of Mermaides.

GIOVANNI
You mean not women I hope Madam?

BELLAURA
Yes.

GIOVANNI
Oh do not by so hard an application
Increase the Poets torment, that first made
That fabulous story to disgrace your sex,
Y'are firm, and the fair seal of the great maker,
A print next that of Angels.

BELLAURA
We are bound t'ee
If our cause want a flourish, you have art
To make us shew fair.

GIOVANNI
And you are so,
'Tis malice dares traduce you; or blind ignorance
That throws her strains, which fall off from your figures,
For those which weaker understandings cal
Your spots, are ermines, and can such as these
Darlings of heaven, and nature, women, shoot
At Court an influence like unlucky planets?
They cannot sure, why you live Madam there,
That are enough to prove all praise, a truth,
And by a sweet example make 'em all
Such as you are objects, of love and wonder,
Oh then how bles't are they that live at Court,
With freedome to converse with so much virtue;
As your fair sex embraceth.

[Enter **URSULA**.

BELLAURA
Here's your mother.

GIOVANNI [aside]
She was too hasty.

URSULA
Madam I hope you'l pardon my sons rudeness
To hold discourse with your Ladiship.

BELLAURA
'Tis a courtesie,
And he talkes well to passe away the time,
Exceeding well, but I must to my Guardian
The Duke—

[Exit.

URSULA
Happinesse attend your Ladiship.
Now sir what are you thinking of?

GIOVANNI
Your pardon, nothing.

[Going.

URSULA
Nay stay, I must talk with you my self,
But first what talk had you with my Lady?

GIOVANNI
She was pleas'd to ask some questions.

URSULA
What were they?

GIOVANNI
I ha' forgot.

URSULA
You ha' forgot y'are a leud
And sawcy boy, go to, your father spoiles you;

[Enter **ROBERTO** and **GEORGIO**.

URSULA
But if you use me sirra 'oth this fashion
I'le break your pate, I will, the Dukes owne sonne
(My blessing upon him) would not answer me
With I ha' forgot, I warrant you, but you—

ROBERTO

Why, how now Vrsula, what? perpetuall clamours?

URSULA
Oh here's your stickler.

GIOVANNI
Nothing unkind to me, she was angry
With your servant Georgio, and threatened to break
His head, away—

GEORGIO
My head? come heels.—

[Exit.

ROBERTO
Was it but so? she shall, she shall do that,
With all my heart, and I will break it too.

URSULA
Nay, then I will be friends with him.

ROBERTO
Where's the knave?

URSULA
I wo'not be compell'd to break his head,
And you were twenty husbands; fare you wel.

ROBERTO
'Tis such a wasp, but she shannot wrong thee.

GIOVANNI
I know she wo'not sir, she is my mother,
She comes agen.

[Enter **URSULA** followed by **THOMAZO, MALIPIERO, BERNADO** and **MARCELLO**.

URSULA
My heart does leap to see you.

ROBERTO
The Dukes son, and a troop of gallants, but
I alwaies have sore eyes to see one there,
That Signior Malipiero, he does owe me
Already forty Crownes, and I forgive him.

MALIPIERO

Signior Roberto, remember that I owe
You forty Crowns.

ROBERTO
Pray, do you forget 'em.

MALIPIERO
I never pay till it come to a hundred.

ROBERTO
Never pay! it is no matter Signior.
I were best be gone before he borrow more,
It is a trick he nses to put on
With his rich clothes, I'le vanish.

[Exit.

MALIPIERO
Strange this English man appears not?

URSULA
I was afraid you had been sick my Lord.

THOMAZO
I was never sick in my life, but when
I had a feaver, or some other infirmity.
I'le call thee nurse stil. Giovanni.

GIOVANNI
Sir.

THOMAZO
Thou lookest like a changling.

GIOVANNI
The more's my misfortune.
You are the Dukes son.

[Exit.

THOMAZO
Who can help it? nurse,

URSULA
He was never courteous to women.
Here's a gentleman, and they talk of a gentleman,
Now could I weep for joy. I must take my leave sir.

THOMAZO
I must make bold with my nurse.

URSULA
Blessings upon thy heart, how sweetly he kisses.
Here was a touch for a Lady.

[Exit.

THOMAZO
Go thy waies,
An admirable twanging lip, pitty thou art
A thought too old: ha wagtaile!

BERNADO
Does he come alone?

MALIPIERO
Alone, be you resolute
When you see me draw, shoot all your points
Into his heart.

BERNADO
Be confident.

MARINO
Unlesse
He be steel-proof, he shannot boast abroad
Much victory in Venice.

[Enter **FLORELLI**, and **GIOVANNI**.

GIOVANNI
Signior Thomazo sir, is there.

FLORELLI
I thank you.

GIOVANNI
You pay too much sir for no service.

THOMAZO
Here he is.
We were wagering thou wouldst not keepe thy promise.

FLORELLI
I durst not make that forfeit of your grace,
I most consult my own, when I am careful

To wait upon your honor.

MALIPIERO
You are noble.

FLORELLI
Your humble servant gentlemen.

THOMAZO
Where didst supp?

FLORELLI
I was not willing to engage my self
Abroad, lest I might trespasse on your patience.

THOMAZO
What shall's do this evening?

MALIPIERO
Walk a turn,
And then to a bona roba.

BERNADO
A match.

THOMAZO
Giovanni!
Thy spade, and hold my cloak.

MALIPIERO
What's the device?

THOMAZO
I have 'great mind to dig now, do'st think I cannot
Handle a spade, i'le make a bed with my Gentlemen now
For a hundred Duccats.

MALIPIERO
'Tis a base employment,
Fit for such a drudge as Giovanni.

GIOVANNI
Sir!

MALIPIERO
A drudge? I said, dee scorne your little dunghill breed?

GIOVANNI

This is not noble.

MALIPIERO
How mole-catcher?

FLORELLI
Forbear he is not arm'd.

MALIPIERO
You were best be his champion.

[**MALIPIERO**, **BERNADO** and **MARINO** draw their swords; **FLORELLI** stands on his defence.

THOMAZO
Are you good at that?
I do not love to wear my doublet pink'd.

[Exit.

GIOVANNI
Three against one?

[**GIOVANNI** recovers a sword, having first us'd his spade to side with the **ENGLISHMAN**: **BERNADO** having lost his weapon flies.

MALIPIERO
Hold.

GIOVANNI
I am no drudg you'll find
To be commanded sir, you painted flies,
And only fit for trouts.

FLORELLI
Let's give 'em play, and breath.

MALIPIERO
Lost our advantage? is Thomazo fled?

MARINO
And Bernardo, we were best retire, that Gardiner
Will stick me into ground, else for a plant.

[Exit.

MALIPIERO
Expect wee'l be reveng'd.

[Exit.

GIOVANNI
Let's prevent 'm.

FLORELLI
They are not worth it Giovanni, so
I heard you nam'd.

GIOVANNI
My name is Giovanni.

FLORELLI
Thou hast reliev'd, and sav'd my life, I find
Their base conspiracie, what shall I pay
Thy forward rescue?

GIOVANNI
'Tis but what I owe
To justice, with the expence of blood and life
To prevent treachery, reward I have
Receiv'd i'th act, if I have done you service.
But 'twas your innocence that made such hast
To your own valour, not my sword preserv'd you.
I am young, and never taught to fight.

FLORELLI
I prethee
Accept this trifle, buy a sword, and wear it,
Thou hast deserv'd to thrive a nobler way
Then thy condition shewes.

GIOVANNI
Though some would call
This bounty, urge it not to my disgrace,
I scorn to sell the motion of my arme!
I fear you are not safe yet, there may be
Danger in following them, and it grows dark.
Have patience while I fetch a key, that shall
Befriend you with a private way.

[Exit.

FLORELLI
Th'art noble,
Though I am carelesse where the termes of honor
Engage my life, 'tis wisdome not to lose it
Upon their base revenge, but I must study

Some other payment for this young mans courage.
How ere his body suffer in a cloud,
His spirit's not obscure, but brave, and active.

[Enter **CORNARI** and several **BRAVO'S** arm'd.

CORNARI
If my intelligence faile not, he must be
Here still. This evening hath put on a Vizard
To conspire with me, there he walkes, surprize him.
They seize upon him, bind his armes and feet, and blind him with a bagg.

FLORELLI
Villaines, Cowards, Slaves, my sword.

BRAVO
If you be lowd, wee'l strange you.

CORNARI
Dispatch.

BRAVO
We ha done sir, is he for the river now?

CORNARI
No, follow me.

[Exeunt with **FLORELLI**.

[Enter **GIOVANNI**.

GIOVANNI
These shew like officers,
Alas hee's apprehended on their base
Complaint, I cannot help; thy cause and innocence
Must now befriend thee! base world! yet I may
Injure, the parts abroad; 'tis onely Venice
Is sick with these distempers, then▪ i'le leave it,
And instantly pursue some other fate
I'th warrs, it may cure something too within me,
That is deny'd all remedy at home,
Some bodies for their Physick, are design'd
To change of aire, i'le try't upon my mind.

[Exit.

SCENE I

The Rialto.

Enter **MALIPIERO** and **THOMAZO**.

THOMAZO
Not this Englishman to be found?

MALIPIERO
He's not above ground
Where I could suspect him in the City—

THOMAZO
Let him go, may be his hast toppled him
Into the river, and we may eat his nose
In the next haddock.

MALIPIERO
Wherefore did you fly?

THOMAZO
Do'st think 'twas fear?

MALIPIERO
'Twas something like a will,
To keep your skin from oilet-holes.

THOMAZO
I grant you,
What had I to do to bring up a fashion?

MALIPIERO
We might ha'gone a sure and nearer way
To ha' kill'd him in a right line with a bullet,
But let him goe, so he quit Venice any way.

THOMAZO
He would spoile our mirth, but I much wonder
Bernardo is not come yet, whom I sent
Embassador for money to the Merchants.

MALIPIERO
Nor Marcello, whom I employ'd to the same end,
To my most Costive Uncle for some goldfinches.

THOMAZO

Why should the state have an Exchequer, and
We want?

MALIPIERO

For pious uses too, to drink their health;
And see the Common-wealth go round
In mutuall commerce of mirth and spirit,
Which phlegme and usury hath almost stifled,
Sobriety and long gownes spoile the City.
'Tis we would keep the body politick
From stinking, ulcer'd with long obligations,
And notaries, which now stuffe the Rialto,
And poyson honest natures, that would else
Live freely, and be drunk at their own charge.

THOMAZO

I would make new lawes, and I were Duke of Venice.

MALIPIERO

We would not sit i'th chimney corner then,
And sing like Crickets.

THOMAZO

We would roare like Trumpets,
And deaf the Senators with, give us your monies—

MALIPIERO

Their's? give us our own, their states, their wives,
And wardrobes Scanderbeg.

THOMAZO

And their pretty daughters,
My valiant Turk, who should feed high o' purpose—

MALIPIERO

To keep the wanton blood in titillations.

THOMAZO

It should be a Law, no maid should be in fashion.

MALIPIERO

Yes let 'em be in fashion, but not hold.

THOMAZO

Not after fourteen be it then enacted.

MALIPIERO

Wee would banish all the Advocates that refus'd
To pimp, and prove it Civill Law.

THOMAZO
No scribe should dare to shew his ears in our Dominions

MALIPIERO
Hang 'em, they are labells of the Law, and stinke,
Worse then a fish-shambles in lent. No Iew
Should turn a Christian upon perill of
A Confiscation.

THOMAZO
Why?

MALIPIERO
The slaves are rich,
To turn 'em Christians were to spoile their Conscience,
And make 'em hide their mony, 'tis lesse evill
In state to cherish Iewes, then Christian Usurers.

THOMAZO
I will have every Citizen a Jew then.

MALIPIERO
We have built no Seraglio yet.

THOMAZO
That's true,
What think you of the Universities?
Would not they serve?

MALIPIERO
O excellent,
They have severall schooles for severall games.

THOMAZO
And scaffolds
For the spectators when we keep our acts.

MALIPIERO
The Colledge rents would find the wenches petticoates,
And the revenues of a score of Abbies
Wel stript; would serve to rowl 'em in clean linnen,
And keep the toyes in diet.

THOMAZO
Excellent!

But when we have converted to the use
The Monasteries, where shall we bestow
The Fryers, and the thin religious men?

MALIPIERO
You may
Keep them with little charge, water is all
The blessing their poor thirst requires, and taylors
Wo'not be troubled for new clothes, a hair shirt
Will outwear a Copy-hold, and warm lives,
Or if you think 'em troublesome, it is
A fair pretence to send 'em to some wild
Country to plant the faith, and teach the infidells
A way to Heaven, for which they may be burn't
Or hang'd, and there's an end o'th honest men.
There be a thousand waies to quiet them.

THOMAZO
My admirable Counsellor, thou shouldst be
My supreme officer to see Justice done.

MALIPIERO
You cannot honour men of worth too much.

THOMAZO
Wee'l ha the bridges all pull'd down, and made
Of silver.

MALIPIERO
Drosse! Gold is our orient metall.

[Enter **BERNADO**.

Here is Bernardo, welcome, where's the money?

BERNADO
Not a gazet: the merchants are all sullen,
And say you owe too much already.

MALIPIERO
These are Dogbolts.
'Tis time we had new lawes and they wo'not trust.

THOMAZO
But we must build
No golden bridges at this rate with sun-beames.

MALIPIERO

They were best content themselves with honest stone,
Hard as the heart of your ungodly Merchants.

THOMAZO
Prethee let's leave our dream of frighting Sailors,
And say, what hope hast thou of getting money
For this daies mirth?

MALIPIERO
Some hope there is, if my Uncle have but faith
Enough, to credit what I never mean,
Thrift and submission, and holy matters;
'Tis all the waies are left to cozen him
And creep into his nature, I have pawn'd
All my religion that il'e turne Fryer.

THOMAZO
Hast pawn'd thy religion, much good do him,
Let him take the forfeit, so he send thee money—

MALIPIERO
For present use, and howl, and hang himself.
I care not—oh—here's Marcello.

[Enter **MARCELLO**.

Didst speak with him?

MARINO
Yes.

MALIPIERO
That's well.

MARINO
He doe's commend him to you, and with it this—

MALIPIERO
I knew t'would take, his tender conscience

THOMAZO
Hast thou prevail'd?

MARINO
This halter—he ha's tyed the knot himself,
And saies next the Philosophers stone, hee knowes not
What thing of nobler value to present you:
And rather then you should delay for want

Of a convenient—you know what, you should
Once more peruse his Orchard, there's one tree
He would have bear no other fruit.

MALIPIERO
I thank him.
For his fine noose, would I had his neck in't,
The Devill should not conjure him from this circle.
Is this the end of all?

THOMAZO
No, not of all.

MALIPIERO
I pretheee try how it will hold—d'ee hear
Let's lay our heads together. Which of you
Is best acquainted with the Turk?

THOMAZO
What Turk.

MALIPIERO
The great and mighty Sultan, the grand Signior.
Or have you but a Christian correspondence
With any of his heathen officers.

THOMAZO
What to do?

MALIPIERO
No rogue that lies purdue here for intelligence?

BERNADO
What then?

MALIPIERO
I would make a bargain with him now and sell
This City to the Pagan instantly.
Venice is a Jewell, a rich pendant;
Would hang rarely at the great Turkes eare.

THOMAZO
No doubt.

MALIPIERO
Or at one horne of his half Moon.

MARINO

I think so.

MALIPIERO
I would betray if I knew how, the state
Or any thing for half a hundred Duccats
To make one merry night, though after I
Were broke upon a wheel, or set upright
To peep through a cleft tree like a pole-cat
In the high way—no money from the Mungrells?
Well if I live. I will to Amsterdam,
And add another schism to the two hundred
Fourscore and odd;
I am resolv'd.

THOMAZO
What?

MALIPIERO
To cry down all things
That hang on wit, truth, or religion.

THOMAZO
Come, thou art passionate, is there no trick?
No lewd device? let me see?—I have thought
Away to raise us my dear Tully, a project
Shall raise us, or i'le venture—

MALIPIERO
What?

THOMAZO
My neck
For hanging is the end of my device,
Unlesse I thrive in't: go to the randevouz,
To Rosabella's O' the grand Cavale,
Kiss her and call for wines, my bullyrookes,
A dish of dainty fidlers to curvet too,
And drink a health that I may prosper, tumble
And shake the house, I'le fetch you off.

MALIPIERO
But fignior—

THOMAZO
No more words, cannot you be gone, be drunk,
And leave me to the reckoning, i'le return
With Indian spoiles like Alexander.

[Exit.

MALIPIERO
Spoken
Like a true Macedonian, we are gone.
He's right, and may in time, and our good breeding
Be brought to something, may deserve the Gallies.
Follow your leaders Mirmidons.

BOTH
We attend.

[Exeunt.

The Duke's Gardens.

[Enter **GIOVANNI** and **GEORGIO**.

GEORGIO
But will you venture Signior Giovanni
Your body to the warrs indeed?

GIOVANNI
I mean so.

GEORGIO
And leave me to be lost, or thrown away
Among the weeds here!

GIOVANNI
Try thy fortune wo'me.

GEORGIO
Yes, and come hopping home upon one legg.
Will all my pay then buy a handsome halter
To hang my arm in, if it be but maim'd,
Yet I endure a battail every day,
My mistris hath a mouth carries whole Cannon;
And if you took that engine to the warrs,
You would find it do rare service.

GIOVANNI
What?

GEORGIO

Her tongue;
Make her but angry, and you'l need no more
Artillery to scoure them with a breach.
What spoile her breath would make in a market place?

GIOVANNI

Be lesse satyricall;
I must not hear this, she is my mother.

GEORGIO

She is my mistris, and thats worse, but I`me resolv'd,
I'le to the warrs w'e, do not tell her on't,
My prentiship is worse then killing there.
My hand, i'le w'ee.

GIOVANNI

In the mean time buy yee a sword, and belt,
And what is fit.

[Gives him money.

GEORGIO

No more, i'le be a souldier;
And kill according to my pay, this will
Suffice to vamp my body, I may rise
If I grow rich in valour, that will do't,
Money and a tilting feather make a Captain.

[Exit.

GIOVANNI

There is no other way to quiet the
Afflictions here, beside 'tis honorable,
And warre a glorious mistris.

[Enter **BELLAURA**, and **ROBERTO**.

'Tis Bellaura and my Father.

ROBERTO

I know Madam you may break his resolution,
If you be pleas'd, you may command; he's here.

BELLAURA

I'le try my skill.

ROBERTO

Blessings attend your Ladiship.
I'le waite for the successe.

[Exit.

BELLAURA
How now Giovanni,
What with a sword, you were not us'd to appeare
Thus arm'd, your weapon is a spade I take it.

GIOVANNI
It did become my late profession Madam;
But I am chang'd.

BELLAURA
Not to a souldier.

GIOVANNI
It is a title Madam will much grace me,
And with the best collection of my thoughts
I have ambition to the warre.

BELLAURA
You have?

GIOVANNI
Oh 'tis a brave profession, and rewards
All losse wee meet with double weight in glory,
A calling Princes stil are proud to own,
And some do willingly forget their crownes
To be commanded, 'tis the spring of all
We here entitle fame to, Emperors
And all degrees of honors, owing all
Their names to this imployment, in her vast
And circular embraces holding Kings,
And making them; and yet so kind as not
To exclude such private things as I, who may
Learn and commence in her great arts. My life
Hath been too uselesse to my self and Country,
'Tis time I should imploy it to deserve
A name within their Registry, that bring
The wealth, the harvest home of well bought honor.

BELLAURA
It is an active time I must confess,
And the unhappy scene of war too nere us
But that it should enflame you on the suddain
To leave a calm, and secure life, is more

Then commonly it workes on men of your
Birth, and condition, besides I hear
Your Father is not willing you should leave him,
To engage your self in such apparent danger.
Here you will forfeit your obedience
Unless you stay.

GIOVANNI
I cannot despair Madam
Of his consent, and if by my own strength
Of reason I incline him not, it was
In my ambition to address my humble
Suite to your Ladiship to gain it for me,
At worst it is no breach of duty Madam,
If I preferr my Country and her cause
Now bleeding, before any formal ties
Of nature to a soft indulgent father.
For danger, let pale soules consider it,
It is beneath my fears.

BELLAURA
Yet I can see
Through all this resolution iovanni?
'Tis somthing else hath wrought this violent chang,
Pray let me be of counsel with your thoughts,
And know the serious motive, come be clear,
I am no enemy, and can assist
Where I allow the cause.

GIOVANNI
You may be angry
Madam, and chide it as a sawcy pride
In me to name, or look at honor, nor
Can I but know what small addition
Is my unskilfull arme to aide a Country.

BELLAURA
I may therefore justly suspect, there is
Something of other force that moves you to
The warrs, enlarge my knowledge with the secret.

GIOVANNI
At this command I open my heart, Madam,
I must confesse there is another cause
Which I dare not in obedience
Obscure, since you will call it forth, and yet
I know you will laugh at me.

BELLAURA
It would ill
Become my breeding Giovanni.

GIOVANNI
Then,
Know Madam, I'm in love.

BELLAURA
In love with whom?

GIOVANNI
With one I dare not name, shee's so much
Above my birth and fortunes.

BELLAURA
I commend
Your flight, but does she know it?

GIOVANNI
I durst never
Appear with so much boldnesse to discover
My hearts so great ambition, 'tis here still,
A strange and busie guest.

BELLAURA
And you think absence
May cure this wound.

GIOVANNI
Or death.

BELLAURA
I may presume,
You think shee's fair.

GIOVANNI
I dare as soon question your beauty Madam,
The onely ornament, and starre of Venice,
Pardon the bold comparison, yet there is
Something in you resembles my great mistris

[She blushes—

Such very beames dispearseth her bright eye
Powerfull to restore decrepit nature,
But when she frownes, and changes from her sweet
Aspect (as in my fears I see you now

Offended at my boldnesse) she does blast
Poor Giovanni thus, and thus I wither
At heart, and wish my self a thing lost in
My own forgotten dust, but it's not possible
At last (if any starres blesse but high thoughts)
By some desert in war, and deeds of honor.)
(For mean as I, have rais'd themselves to Empire)
That she without a blush to stain her cheek
May own me for a servant—I am lost
In wandring apprehensions.

BELLAURA
Poor Giovanni,
I pitty thee, but cannot cure—I like
Thy aspiring thoughts, and to this last of love,
Allow the warrs a noble remedy.

[Enter **ROBERTO** and **URSULA**.

I have argu'd against your son's resolve, but find
His reasons overcome my weak dispute.
And I must counsell you to allow 'em too.

URSULA
Nay, I was never much against it Madam.

ROBERTO
She loves him not, but does your Ladiship
Think fitting, he should go?

BELLAURA
Yes, yes 'tis honorable;
And to encourage his forward spirit,
The Generall is my kinsman Giovanni,
What favours he can do you, you shall have
My letters to entreat, and at my charge
You shall be furnish'd like a Gentleman,
Attend me at my lodgings.

GIOVANNI
You bind all
My services; why this will make a shew yet.

ROBERTO
Nay, then take my consent and blessing too.

URSULA
And mine: the Duke.

[Exeunt **GIOVANNI**, **ROBERTO** and **URSULA**.

[Enter **DUKE** and **MARINO**.

DUKE
Bellaura, I must speak to you.

BELLAURA
I attend.

DUKE
You have my purpose, and return me clearly
How he bestowes himself, and what society
Withdrawes him from his duty thus.

MARINO
I shall
With my best care.

DUKE
I fear that Malipiero,
But let me find your diligence: Bellaura.

[Exit with **BELLAURA** followed by **MARINO**.

SCENE III

A Gallery in Cornari's House.

The Scene adorn'd with Pictures amongst the rest Claudiana's. Enter **BRAVOS** with the **ENGLISHMAN**,
they unbind him and exeunt.

FLORELLI
I am all wonder: shall I trust my sences.
A fair and pleasant gallery; was I
Surpriz'd for this? or do I dream, I did
Expect the end of my conveyance should
Have been more fatal,

[Looks around.

No tract appears, or signe of those that brought me,
The place is rich in ornament, sure these
Are Pictures, all things silent as the Images,
And yet these speak, some do inhabit here,

This room was not ordain'd onely for air
And shadowes, 'tis some flattering Prologue to
My death, some plot to second the affront
Of Malipiero with more scorne to ruine me.

[Enter **CORNARI** masked and disguised, with a case of Pistols.

What art?

CORNARI
A friend.

FLORELLI
That posture and presentment
Promise no great assurance, yet there's something
Within that noble frame would tempt me to
Believe thou art.

CORNARI
What?

FLORELLI
A black murderer.
Point not thy horrid messengers of death
Upon a man disarm'd, my bosome is
No proof against those fiery Executioners.
How came I to deserve from thee unknown
So black a purpose, as thy lookes present me?
I never saw thy face, nor am I conscious
Of any act, in whose revenge, thou hast
Put on this horror, let me know my guilt
Before I die, although I never liv'd
At that poor rate to fear a noble death;
Yet unprepar'd, and thus to die, doth something
Stagger my soul, and weaken my resolve
To meet thy Execution, thou hast
Too good a face to be a Mercenary
Cut-throat, and Malipiero would become
The hangmans office better.

CORNARI
You believe then,
How easily I can command your destine,
I have no plot with any Malipiero,
And thus remove thy fears

[Exits with the Pistols.

FLORELLI
Is he gone?

[Re-enter **CORNARI**.

CORNARI
Y'are still within
My power, but call your selfe my guest, not prisoner,
And if you be not dangerous to your self
Nothing is meant but safety here and honor.

FLORELLI
This does amaze me more; but do Italians
Compell men to receive their courtesies?

CORNARI
I must not give you reasons; yet for your
Surprize, you may receive a timely knowledge
And not repent. I am a Gentleman,
And by that name secure thee, if you can
Fancie a peace with this restraint, 'tis none
But something that may please you above freedom,
If your unruly thoughts tempt a resistance,
Death is let in, at every thing you look at.

FLORELLI
I'le leave my wonder and believe, what now
Must I obey?

CORNARI
First walk away your fright.

FLORELLI
'Tis off.

CORNARI
How do you like this gallery?

FLORELLI
'Tis very handsome.

CORNARI
And these pictures.

FLORELLI
Wel.

CORNARI

Your eyes are yet too carelesse, pray examine 'em.

FLORELLI
They cannot answer.

CORNARI
Now your opinion.

FLORELLI
Very good faces.

CORNARI
Have your eyes ever
Met with a substance that might reflect
On any of these shadowes sir in Venice?

FLORELLI
Never.

CORNARI
Look a little better, is there nothing
Of more then common curiosity,
In any of these beauties.

FLORELLI
I have seen
Fair ones, what should this mean?

CORNARI
But pray tel me,
Of these (which some have prais'd for handsomness)
Which doth affect you most? I guesse you have
By frequent view, and the converse with Ladies
Ariv'd at excellent judgement:

FLORELLI
I did not
Expect this Dialogue, yet i'le be free,
I profess stranger to 'em all, but this

[Pointing to **CLAUDIANA'S** portratit.

I should elect the fairest and most worthy
A masculine Embrace. I build upon
The promise of your Honour, I should else
Be nice in my opinion.

CORNARI

You are just,
And I prefer that too, what will you say
To call that Lady Mistris, and enjoy her?
Shee's noble to my knowledge, but enough
At this time. I must pray your kind excuse
If whilst you walk into this room

[Opening the hanging.

FLORELLI
A fair one.

CORNARI
Which is design'd your lodging, I become
Your jailour, and make sure this Gallery
Til my return; be constant to your temper,
There shall be nothing wanting to procure
You safe, and pleasant hours.

FLORELLI
Distrust falles off.
I will expect to find you noble, though
My faith bind not to all, and enter.

[Exit.

CORNARI
So.
I tread a maze too, but must not resign
My office, till I perfect my design

[Exit.

SCENE IV

A Room in Rosabella's House.

[Enter **MALIPIERO** with **ROSABELLA** dancing; **BERNADO** and **MARCELLO**.

BERNADO
Active Malipiero.

MARINO
Excellent!
They move as they had nothing else but soul.

MALIPIERO
So, drink, we are not merry, here's a health
To my hen sparrow.

MARINO
Let it walk round.

BERNADO
What Rosabella's health? before the states—

MALIPIERO
Hang States, and Commonwealths we will be Emperors;
And laugh, and drink away whole Provinces.
Shall we not didapper?

ROBERTO
What you please, but will Signior
Thomazo be here presently, and bring—

MALIPIERO
The golden Fleece, thou Lady Guinever,
And he shall mount thy little modesty,
And ride like Agamemnon, and shall pay for't,
While we, like valiant Greekes in lusty wine,
Drench the remembrance that we are mortal,
More wine, my everlasting Marmoset.

BERNADO
Brave Malipiero still! our grand Signiors health!

[Drinks.

Signior Thomazo.

MALIPIERO
Let it come squirrells,
And then a song my pretty Rosabella,
Which of the Senators were here last night
To court thee with a draught of dissolv'd pearle?
Be supple to thy friends, and let thy men
Of state, who hide their warp't leggs in long gowns,
And keep their wisdom warm in furrs like agues,
Most grave and serious follies, wait, and want
The knowledge of thy fidle, my dear Dowsabel.

ROBERTO
What hath advanc'd your brain thus Malipiero?
You were not wont to talk at such a height,

There is some mighty fortune drpoping, is
Your Uncle sick, whose heir you hope to be?

MALIPIERO
Hang Uncles, there's a damp in's very name.
Wine, or I sink,—so now thy song, come sit.

[**ROSABELLA** sings.

[Enter **THOMAZO** with **MARINO**.

THOMAZO
Nay you shall enter, Gentlemen, my friend, Salute him, Malipiero, he is one
May do us service.

MARINO
Sir! i'le take my leave.

THOMAZO
That were a jest, you shall stay by this hand,
Who ha's the wine, drink to my noble friend,
Whilst I embrace my Queen of Carthage.

ROBERTO
Welcome.

MALIPIERO
I have seen this Gentleman wait nere your Father.

THOMAZO
Right in his bedchamber, a sober Coxcombe,
We met by chance, let's make him drunk, I have
The brave devices here boy.

MALIPIERO
Good: y'are welcome,
Fill me a ton of wine.

MARINO
How Signior!

MALIPIERO
It is too too little for a friend.

MARINO [aside]
They'l drown me, here's a precious knot

THOMAZO

I hugge thee Cleopatra, Gentlemen,
Am not I behind half a score glasses, fil,
Come charge me home, i'le take it here

[He takes the bottle and drinks.

MARINO
What will become of me? they mean to drench
Me for the sullens, I am like to have
A very fine time, and employment here.

THOMAZO
But ha'you nere a banquet?

ROSABELLA
'Tis preparing.

THOMAZO
Let it be as rich as the Egyptian Queen
Made for Mark Anthony; in the mean time
What limb of wantonnesse have you ready for
My noble friend here, get him a fine flesh saddle,
Or where's thy mother, now I think upon't,
He loves to ride upon a pad.

MARINO
Not I sir.

MALIPIERO
Oh by all meanes Signior.
He shall go to the price of any Ladyware.

MARINO
Who I? alas my tilting daies are done, nay, nay, then
I'le drink w'ee gentlemen, but I cannot tumble

THOMAZO
Why then here's to thee.

MARINO
No Lady ware for me sweet Mistris,
I blush to say I cannot mount at this time.

[Exit **ROSABELLA**.

Would I were off agen, polecats for me?

THOMAZO

Now gentlemen wipe your eyes

[Shewes a Cabinet.

MARINO
A Cabinet of rich Jewels.

THOMAZO
And how, and how shew things?
Is't fit we want to revel, while my father
Ha's these toyes idle, we grope in the dark
And lose our way, while such bright starres as these
May light us to a wench?

MARINO
There is no conscience in't.
But what shall we do with 'em? there's a lustre
Hath struck me into a flame.

MALIPIERO
Drink half, and tumble out the rest
In featherbeds.

THOMAZO
Where's Rosabella, to lend money?

MARINO
Stay, sir,
She never can disburse to half their valew,
Beside I know their slie and costive natures.
I am acquainted with a Jew, are we
All faithfull? are there no traitors here?
I am acquainted with a Jew shall furnish you
To purpose, & transport these, where they shannot
Betray from whence they came: trust her? 'tis dangerous,
Besides the scanting of your mirth, by a
Penurious Son, give me the Cabinet—
Y'are sure all these are friends, & will say nothing?

THOMAZO
I warrant thee; what luck had I to meet him.

MALIPIERO
Will you trust him?

THOMAZO
He's one of us, make hast, a mighty sum.

MARINO
I'le bring a storm of Duccats instantly.

[Exit, with the cabinet.

THOMAZO
So, so to'th wine agen.

MALIPIERO
You need not spend the total here, I have use
For forty of those Duccats.

THOMAZO
S'hat have fifty.

MALIPIERO
These gentlemen are out of figleaves too.
Some fresher robes would shew well.

THOMAZO
They shall have
New skins my Holofernes.

MALIPIERO
I'le have half.

BERNARDO & MARINO
A match.

MALIPIERO
Wine, to our Generalissimo!

[Drinks.

THOMAZO
That's I, I understand the Metaphor.
It shall have law, oh for some trumpets now.

MALIPIERO
Tantarra rara boyes, outrore the winds
And drink the sun into Eclipse, hang miching,
But where's my wanton Pinnace?

BERNADO
Boarded by.
Some man of war by this time.

MARINO

She is spoon'd away.

MALIPIERO
My top and top gallant gone? ha! are there Pirates
Upon these Goasts; give fire upon the water-rats,
And shoot pell mell, fight as a whirlewind flinges,
Disordering all, what man of Menaces
Dare look awry upon my Cattamountaine?

THOMAZO
Not I: now hee's got rampant, heel kill some body.

BERNADO
You must not be affrighted, to'ther lift
And be a Giant eke, and talk of terrors
With words Olympus high.

THOMAZO
Will that do't?

BERNADO
Oh sir.

THOMAZO
Give me the bottle then?

[Drinks.

MALIPIERO
Suppose thou wert my Uncle now, come hither,
Hold thy head fair, that I may whip it off.

MARINO
Mine's nothing like, Bernardo has been taken
For your Uncle Signior.

MALIPIERO
How dare you be like
The rogue my Uncle sirra?

BERNADO
I sir? 'tis
Signior Thomazo that he means, and see
For very fear his head falls off

[**THOMAZO** was drinking and here sets down the bottle.

MALIPIERO

Reach it me,
I'le drink a health, then in his skull.

THOMAZO
Who talkes of me, who dares mention
A thought of me? where be the dainty duccats?

[Enter **MARINO**.

MARINO
The moneie's coming sir, six men are laden,
And will be here immediately.

MALIPIERO
Thou shalt drink
A health, kneel venerable sir.

THOMAZO
Be humble,
Thou man of Malligo, or thou dyest

MARINO
I do sir.

[Kneels.

MALIPIERO
To the Town, a fire.

MARINO
What dee mean Signior.

THOMAZO
He has a very good meaning, never doubt it.

MALIPIERO
That you shall pledge, or forfeit your sconce to me,
None shall have the honor to pledge this health,
But this whey-bearded Signior.

THOMAZO
Now do my braines tumble, tumble, tumble—

MALIPIERO
Give it him,
And drink it with devotion as I did.

[**MARINO** drinks.

THOMAZO
I long to see these double, double—

[Hiccups.

But where's the Cockatrice, this whirligigge?
Is my head fast?

MARINO
The scrue is firm, suspect not.

MARINO [aside]
I dare not pray nor ask forgivenesse here.

THOMAZO
Do not my braines now turn upon the toe.

MALIPIERO
Do you hear my doughty Signior Thomazo,
Won't you kill the Duke, your graceless father now?

THOMAZO
Yes marry will I.

MALIPIERO
You sha'l let him into the Chamber one night,
Where he shall strangle him [To **MARINO**].

THOMAZO
O! I can play upon his windpipe rarely.

MALIPIERO
We'll see d'ee mark some corner of the Palace
A fire, at the same time, and in that hurry
Break into the Treasury, take what we think fit,
And steal away by Sea into another Country.

MARINO
Most admirably contriv'd; the men are come.

[Enter **OFFICERS**, armed.

THOMAZO
Hey, the money boyes?

MARINO
Disarme the traitors.

MALIPIERO
Plots, ambuscadoes, are these your Jew tricks.

MARINO
I'll wait till you have slept away your surfeit,
Here in the house.

THOMAZO
Which is the Jew of all these?

MALIPIERO
We are cheated by a Court-nap.

THOMAZO
My friend, are you the Jew? where be the Jewells.

MARINO
Truth is, I have sent the Jewels to your Father,
And he will lend no money.

THOMAZO
No money?

MALIPIERO
But must we go to prison?

THOMAZO
I'le to prison with e'm spight o' your teeth.

MARINO
Not, till you have slept, this way.

[Exit. with **THOMAZO**

[Enter **ROSABELLA**.

ROBERTO
The Banquet's ready gentlemen.

MALIPIERO
A rescue.
We are snatch'd up for traitors, we are betraid,
And going to prison.

ROBERTO
Who paies for the wine and banquet?

MALIPIERO
Why any living body, that has a scruple
In's Conscience, for the losse of thy dear Comfits,
And Carrawaies, away, lead me ye rogues.
'Ie not march else, and let us make a shew,
My fine officious rascalls, on afore,
I follow in fit state, so farewell firelock.

ROSABELLA
I shall be undone.

MALIPIERO
Undoing is thy trade,
March on I say.

[Exeunt.

ACT IV

SCENE I

A Room in Cornari's House.

Enter **CORNARI**, after him **CLAUDIANA**.

CLAUDIANA
Your pleasure sir; you did command my presence.

CORNARI
Are you come? you and I must not be
Interrupted, Claudiana.

[Makes fast the door.

CLAUDIANA
Why do you shut your Chamber?

CORNARI
We must be private.
How does my life?

CLAUDIANA
Well sir, if you be so.

CORNARI
I have a sute to thee, my best Caudiana.

CLAUDIANA
To me? it must be granted.

CORNARI
That's well said,
But 'tis a business (sweet) of mighty consequence,
More precious then my life.

CLAUDIANA
Goodness forbid
I should not give obedience to the least
Of your commands, but when your life requires
My service, I should chide my heart, and thoughts
Unless they put on wings to shew their duty.

CORNARI
Nay, 'tis a business sweet will speak thy love.

CORNARI
Thou knowest how many years since the Priest tied
Our holy knot, with what religious flowing
Of chast and noble love our hearts have met,
How many blessings have I summ'd in thee,
And but in thee, for unto this, Heaven gave not
(That which indeed doth Crown all Marriage,)
Children, thou hast been fruitful Claudiana
In all that's good, but onely fruitfulness;
And when I think who in my want of that
Great blessing of thy womb, must be my heir,
A base and impious villain, to possesse
And riot in my spacious fortunes, I
Forget that other happiness in thy person,
And let in a vexation to consume me.

CLAUDIANA
I know not what to fear, it is heavens will
And not my fault.

CORNARI
Oh no, the fault is mine,
All mine Claudiana, for thou art not barren
'Tis I, a man prodigious and mulcted
By nature, without faculty of man
To make our marriage happy, and preserve
This fair; this lovely figure, be at peace
And let me blush, a thing not worth the love
Of such a bounteous sweetnesse.

[Kneels.

CLAUDIANA
Let me fall
Beneath that which sustaines me, ere I take
In a beleef, that will destroy my peace,
Not in the apprehension of what
You frame to accuse your self, but in fear
My honour is betraid to your suspicion;
Oh kill me sir, before I lose your thought,
Your noble thought.

CORNARI
Rise, with thy tears I kisse
Away thy tremblings; I suspect thy honor?
My heart will want faith to believe an Angel,
That should traduce thy fair name, thou art chast
As the white down of heaven, whose feathers play
Upon the wings of a cold winters gale,
Trembling with fear to touch the impurer earth.
How are the roses frighted in thy cheekes
To palenesse, weeping out of transparent dew:
When a loose story is but nam'd? thou art
The miracle of a chast wife, from which fair
Original, drawn out by heavens own hand,
To have had one Copie, I had write perfection
To all my wishes here, but 'tis denyed me,
Nor do I mock thee with a fable, while
I miserably complain, convinc'd, and lost
In my own Masculine defect; but yet
I love thee Claudiana, dost not think so?
And after so much injury, I bring
Not my repentance onely, but a just
And noble satisfaction.

CLAUDIANA
You oppresse
My sences with the weight of new amazement.

CORNARI
I must be clear, thou must embrace another—
Another in my bed, whom from the world
I have made choice to know thee, be not frighted
This way is left, and this alone to recompence
My want, and make both happy.

CLAUDIANA

I embrace
Another in your bed?

CORNARI
Dost think I would
Attempt, or wish thee to't, without a care
In every circumstance to both our fames?

CLAUDIANA
Fame? are you master of your reason? dare you
Provoke heaven thus?

CORNARI
Heaven onely shall be witnesse,
Whose secrefie i'le trust, but not anothers.
Beside the principal agent, to get heaven.

CLAUDIANA
Y'are no Italian sure.

CORNARI
Yes, and thy husband,
A just one to thy memory, that would
Cancel his faith, rather then be a strict
Idolater of words, and severe lawes,
To the destroying of so sweet a figure;
I would not have thee fly like birds i'th aire,
Or shippes that leave no tract, to say here was,
So rich a blessing, rather like a plant
Should root, and grow, and bloom, & bear for ever.

CLAUDIANA
I'm lost for ever.

CORNARI
Be wise and meet my wishes, 'tis my love
That hath 'orecome all nice considerings
To do thee justice. Nor will I intrude
Upon thy bosome one shall be unwelcome,
He's honorably born, of comely person,
But has a soule addes glory to 'em both,
A boy from him, born to my name and fortunes
Leaves not another wealth to my ambition.
To raise thy free consent my Claudiana,
'Tis he, Whom thou dost think worth thy owne praise,
The gentleman victorious for his parts,
So late in Venice, the English Cavalier.

CLAUDIANA
I am undone.

CORNARI
To be short,
I have surpriz'd his person for this use,
He hath been many daies an obscure guest
Within the lodgings next the Garden, for
I must confesse I have had struglings in
My nature, and have sate in Councel 'gainst
My selfe sometime, touching this great affair,
But I have answer'd every thing oppos'd it,
And took this time to acquaint thee.

CLAUDIANA
Good sir kill me.

CORNARI
I will,
And him too, if ye mingle not and make
The project as I cast it, be not obstinate,
Why, he shall nere discover who thou act,
If thou be faithfull to thy self, thou maist
Pretend thy self some pleasant bona roba.
Dr take what name, and shape thou wilt.

CLAUDIANA
There's none
Can hide my shame, or wash the stain away:

CORNARI
What shame or stain is in't when it is kept
A secret darker then the book of destinie
From mankind?

CLAUDIANA
Am I practis'd in those arts?
Of sin that he should take me for a Curtesan?
Nay, rather let me be known your wife,
It will oblige him more to use me well,
And thank your loving paines that brought me to him.
If I must be a whore, and you a—

CORNARI
Stay, and I a—what? I bleed within me.

CLAUDIANA
This key will make the Chamber free, I follow.

Consider sir, I'm else undone for ever

[Exit.

CORNARI
Why if he know me for her husband, 'tis
Without a name, I can secure my honor,
And send him quickly to eternall silence.
I'me resolv'd they must obey, proceed,
A little blood will wash away this deed.

[Exit.

An Apartment in the Palace.

[Enter **DUKE, SENATORS, ATTENDANTS;** a table with letters.

DUKE
Our City drooping with the wounds so late
Receiv'd, is now to study with what joyes
To entertain so great a victory.
Treviso is return'd to our obedience,
Almost without a losse, how many fell
On the adverse part, those papers signifie,
And must enlarge our triumph: but is't not
Strange what our general writes of Giovanni,
Whose spirit he admires, and forward valour,
Referring to his bold attempt, our Conquest,
That he advanc'd his head and sword first on
The enemies walls, which inflam'd our army
To second him with courage, and that after
With his own hands he slew their generall,
Whose fall shot death and trembling through their Army.

CANDIANO
Where is Giovanni?

DUKE
He is by direction of our generall
Now marching hither, to his onely conduct.
The Captives are remitted, and his act
By us to be considered, but we have
Sent order for the placing of his Prisoners
Securely, and commanded he should here

Attend our pleasure

CANDIANO
The young Gardiner?

DUKE
The same, whose early valour takes away
The prejudice of humble birth, and ought
To be encourag'd nobly.

CANDIANO
'Tis but justice.

[Enter **MARINO** and whispers to the **DUKE**.

Is't possible the Gardiners Son should so
Behave himself in war,
He will deserve some honor for't.

DUKE
Why may not
Our power dispence, and though his low condition
By our rule exempt him (for his gallant service
Done) now create him gentleman of Venice,
With a noble pension from our treasury
To bear his title up?

CANDIANO
We give it strangers,
Whose birth we not examine,
He deserves it.

DUKE
Let him receive no favour
For his relation to me, but take
His place and punishment with the rest, away
I cast him from my thought.

[Exit **MARINO**.

CANDIANO
Why comes not
Our General himself?

DUKE
Reasons of war
May yet compel his stay, he's to repair
Some breaches which our Souldiers made, & wisely

By some new fortification, secure
The Town if the Enemy should reinforce.

[Enter an **ATTENDANT**.

ATTENDANT
Signior Giovanni waites.

DUKE
Hath he dispos'd
By our direction those prisoners were
Sent by our Generall?

ATTENDANT
He hath and please your excellencie.

DUKE
Admit him.

[Enter **GIOVANNI** plum'd and brave **GEORGIO** his servant

GIOVANNI
All health and honor to the Duke and Senate.

DUKE
We thank thee Giovanni, and will spare
Your trouble to 'relate what we have gain'd
I'th war; Our General writes how much our Venice
Doth owe to you, whose maiden yet bold valour,
Hath wrought our safety, and supprest the late
Insolent Genovese.

GIOVANNI
Your bounty makes
That mine, which I want merit sir to challenge,
But if my will to serve my Country (for
Beside that name and warm desires, I dare
Call nothing mine) y'are pleas'd to accept and cherish
A young mans duty, you will teach me in
The next employment to deserve indeed.
Till when, you lose not, to have built upon
This humble pile, a monument of your goodnesse,
To tell the world, although misplac'd on me,
You love a growing vertue.

DUKE
This Giovanni?
His words tast more of courtier then the Garden.

To shew we understand, and to that knowledge
Have will to recompence the desert, Giovanni
The Senate bids you ask, what in your power
Your thought can aim at, to reward your service,
And you shall soon possesse it.

GEORGIO
Ask, ask quickly,
A hundred thousand double double duccats.
'Twil serve us both, do't, beggars must be impudent.

GIOVANNI
Now you destroy what else might live to serve you,
This grace will make me nothing, when I call
My airy worth to ballance, keep those glorious
Rewards for men borne, and brought up in honor?
That may be great and able Columnes to
Your ever envyed state; alas I rise
Like a thin reede beneath this Common-wealth,
Whose weight, an Atlas must sustain like heaven,
This favour is too mighty, and if you
Command me, ask a just reward, 'tis nothing.

GEORGIO
You had as good ha said nothing, I blush for you,
You know many Souldiers
So modest, to refuse pay, or preferment?
They cannot have it sometimes, after many
Petitions to the State, and now their mindes
Are soluble and apt to powre out favours,
You to be so maidenly—

GIOVANNI
May I credit
With pardon of your wisdomes, that you mean
To encourage thus the low born Giovanni?

GEORGIO
Now he makes question of their honesty too,
Oh simple souldier.

DUKE
We look not at thy root, but at thy blossom,
And as a preserver of our Country
We offer up a gratitude, consult
With thy best judgement, (though beside this act
Of his abroad) I can give no account [Aside]
Why I should love this young man, or prefer him,

I know not by what mystery, I have
Had thoughts to wish him more then common fortune,
And this occasion of his merit offered.
I will pursue.

GEORGIO
Do as I counsel you, and remember, I
Have left my fortunes, and my trade to serve you.

GIOVANNI
Call it not pride if I be willing to
Believe your excellence, that I have done
Something your goodnesse prompts you to reward,
And the grave Senate, I have thought.

DUKE
Be free.

GEORGIO [aside]
Now do I expect to be half a Senator at least.

GIOVANNI
And since you raise my act to such a merit,
I will not ask a thing too much beneath it.

GEORGIO [aside]
Well said Vanni.

GIOVANNI
And shame your bounty; yet I may fear
You will not grant—

GEORGIO [aside]
Agen?

DUKE
Name it with confidence.

GIOVANNI
I look at no reward of gold.

GEORGIO [aside]
How's that? hee's out on's part.

GIOVANNI
I know not,
By what fate I contemn it, nor at titles
Of honor, or command, or what can trench

On state or wealth.

GEORGIO [aside]
I thank yee heartily,
I must to dig agen.

GIOVANNI
Employ such gifts,
To pay some slight, and mercenary soules,
That make their end of good, reward, and not
It selfe, but since you have impos'd I should
Make choyce of somwhat know my ambition aims—

DUKE
At what?

GIOVANNI
It is too great a happinesse, but I now
Consider I have pratled to the wind,
What I desire is not within your power,
And what you may command, not in my wishes,
For I would ask Bellaura: can you make
Me fit for such a blessing? no, you cannot,
Unlesse I were unborn, and should agen
Come forth, not Giovanni, but the Son
Of some bright name, and this world-taking honor.

DUKE
Bellaura? strange request.

[Enter **MARINO** and **BELLAURA**.

MARINO
Madam I dare not
Be seen, if you prevail, I shall attend,
And put his mercy into act.

[Exit.

DUKE
She's here.

BELLAURA
I have a suit to your highnesse.

DUKE
Me Bellaura?

BELLAURA
About your son, whom men to your dishonor
Lead like some base offender.

DUKE
I must speak
The cause into your ear. [Whispers to her]

GIOVANNI
I was too blame
To mention her so publick, but my heart
Grew sick with silence, and their proposition
To ask what I desir'd most, prevail'd
Against my reason:

DUKE
Leave him to me, Bellaura.
Do you observe that gentleman?

BELLAURA
'Tis Giovanni.
He does become the souldier.

DUKE
He has done wonders
Abroad, and quit our gratitude, to be
Only by you rewarded, can you love him?

BELLAURA
I understand you not.

DUKE
And marry him?

BELLAURA
How have I lost my self, since I became
Your charge, a legacie bequeath'd your care
By my dead father, the late Duke of Venice,
That you should think I can descend with such
Forgetfullness of my self, my birth or fortunes
To place my love on one so poorly born.

DUKE
You blush. Bellaura 'tis anger in my blood to hear him nam'd.
[To **GIOVANNI**]
You pay me coursely for my charity.
Learn modesty hereafter to be gratefull.
I ha done with you, sir

[Exit.

GEORGIO
Do you heer the tit? be wise,
And look at ready money, 'tis a better
Commodity then any Lady in Christendom;

GIOVANNI
Pray dismiss,
And pardon Giovanni. I am satisfied.
For your own honor let not my ambition
Be told abroad, i'le check and punish my
Aspiring thoughts hereafter.

DUKE
You have leave,
Come gentlemen,
He is in love.

DUKE
I pitty him.

[Exit **DUKE** and **SENATOR**.

GEORGIO
What shall become of us now by your folly?

GIOVANNI
Wee'l to the Garden George, and there begin
Another grouth, for what we have's despis'd.

GEORGIO
I knew I should return to my dear dunghill.

GIOVANNI
I prethee see the armour which Bellaura
Bestow'd on me, brought home.

GEORGIO
Your armour? yes
We might have worn soft natur'd silk, and you had
Been rul'd by me, a pox of love for my part,
'Tis good for nothing, but to make things dear.

GIOVANNI
I'le be reveng'd upon my starrs, that made
Me poor, and dye forgotten in my shade

[Exit.

SCENE III

The Picture Gallery in Cornari's House.

A Table prepar'd, two tapers. Enter **FLORELLI**.

FLORELLI
I find no great devotion in this
Monastick life, the Maior Domo promis'd
A Mistris here of that complexion,

[Pointing to Claudiana's portrait.

But I like not this solitude,
And tedious expectations,
I shall nere do things handsomly,
Give me freedome and fair play,
And turn me to a harpy, but to be thus
Compell'd to an imbrace (for thats the meaning
Of my slie Signior, if it be not worse)
Fed high to encounter with an Amazon,
I know not? tis not well, nor conscionable
In my opinion: I hear some busie
About the lock.

[Enter **CORNARI**.

My Jaylor? What now fellowes?
Sir, if I must ha my throat cut, as much
Better I do not hope, though I deserve not
That bounty from your hands, I live so dully,
I would request you set a time, and't be
A day or two, to pray and think of matters,
And then turn me loose to the other world!

CORNARI
Read that.

[Gives him a paper]

He shannot see my blushes, I must pitty
Thee Claudiana, but my stubborn fate
Will have it so, it is to make thee live

Although we both must suffer, and I like
A father thus, whose child at play upon
A rivers bank, is faln into the stream,
Leap in, and hazard all to save a little,
But I must on

[Exit.

FLORELLI
Amazement Circles me,
Such wonders are not read in every Marriage,
What shall I doe? madnesse to question it.
I must resolve or die? since there's no help,
Tis something if she be but like that face
To comfort my proceeding.

[Enter **CORNARI** leading **CLAUDIANA**, his wife veiled.

CORNARI
Behold! and take as lent this treasure from me,
I must expect it back agen with interest.

[Locks the door and Exit.

FLORELLI
The dore is fast agen, here is a president
For husbands that want heirs to their estate.
A goodly person. Please you Lady, to
Unveil; a rich and most inviting beauty.

[She unveils.

I am all flame, shall I take boldnesse, after
My duty paid your white hand, to aspire
And touch your lip—now could I wish to dwell here.

[He kisses her.

Can you read Lady?

[She takes the paper & turns.

She turns away her face. I hope my Signior
Has taken pains to bring her to the business,
And not left me to break her: can she speak?
Those lines (I know not how you like 'em Madam)
Were none of my invention, the character,
I guesse to be your husbands. I am here

A prisoner to his will, to which unlesse
You give obedience, I have took leave
Of day for ever, destin'd by his vow
To an eternall shade. She leads the way;

[Exit **CLAUDIANA**.

Conscience be calme, no grumblings now of piety.

[Exit following her.

ACT V

SCENE I

The Duke's Gardens.

The pieces of Armour hung upon several trees.

Enter **GIOVANNI**, **ROBERTO** and **URSULA**.

GIOVANNI
These were the excellent Bellaura's gift,
Of no use now to me, but to keep fresh
The memory of my dreams and that I lov'd her.
I see how passion did blind my reason,
And my prodigious hopes vanish'd to air
Have left me to contemplate my own vanity.

ROBERTO
I know not, but if I may credit Georgio
That did wait on thee to the Senate, thou
Hast lost an opportunity, that might
Have made us all Clarissimo's Giovanni.
I might have kept my reverend Mules, and had
My Crupper worshipped by the Plebeians,
And Ursula here been Madam heaven knowes what,
And did you wisely to refuse?

URSULA
Nay, nay I know
He was not born to do us good, not stoop
To take preferment from the Duke and Senate?

ROBERTO
Well, 'twas his modesty.

URSULA
He learn't it not from me.

ROBERTO
No more—

URSULA
You wil be alwaies taking his part against me,
But I know, what I know, and that's a secret,
Here comes the t'other Dunderhead.

[Enter **GEORGIO**.

GEORGIO
The armour is hung up already, this
We must all come to.

ROBERTO
What to the Gibet Georgio?

[Pointing to the Helmet.

GEORGIO
Master look here.
If you had but this hole to put your head in,
It would be a great preservative to your hearing,
And keep out all the noise, of my Dames Culvering,
Within this fortification well lock'd up.
You would think her loudest scolding a meer whisper.

URSULA
What's that you talk of your Dame sirra?

GEORGIO
Oh dame, I have newes for you.

URSULA
For me? what is't? whom does your new's concern?

GEORGIO
One that you love with all your heart.

ROBERTO
Who is't knave?

GEORGIO
Knave? call your word in, and eat it, I'le advise,

You may fare worse: you do not hear the news then?

URSULA
I shall when you'l find utterance.

GEORGIO
The newes—
We are all of one Religion?

ROBERTO
Out with it.

GEORGIO
Every thing is not to be talk'd on.

ROBERTO
So it seems by your concealment.

URSULA
Shall we hear it?

GEORGIO
Yes? Signior Thomazo—

URSULA
What of him?

GEORGIO
There's a gentleman, and you talk of a gentleman.

URSULA
What of Thomazo? now am I longing.

GEORGIO
I heard, as I came hither—

URSULA
What?

ROBERTO
Let us hear too.

URSULA
What? be brief.

GEORGIO
That he is to lose his head Mistriss—

URSULA

Now a thousand blisters upon that tongue.

GEORGIO

But you do not know for what, mistrisse there's it,
You are so angry still at half a businesse.

URSULA

For what is he to suffer? oh my heart!

GEORGIO

For nothing but high treason.

ROBERTO

How?

GEORGIO

You ha'not patience, to hear a story out.

ROBERTO

High treason said he? that's a shrewd business.

URSULA

Thomazo lose his head?

ROBERTO

So it seems.

URSULA

Better thy generation were headlesse.

GEORGIO

I told you but in good will, because I knew
You lov'd him. I have done.

[Exit.

URSULA

Passion O my dear heart! i'le to the Duke
My self, and beg his pardon.

ROBERTO

You'll make
Your self a party in the treason, will you?
You'l beg his pardon, you'l beg a halter,
And sooner 'twill be granted.

URSULA

Giovanni,
Sweet Giovanni, there's a sunshine word,
Deere child go with us.

ROBERTO
Us? dost think i'le goe
And run my head into the hempe?

URSULA
Best hony-suckle!
One word ohine will strike the pardon dead.

GIOVANNI
Ide rather go a pilgrimage.

[Exit.

URSULA
Thou shalt go a pilgrimage, another time
To the worlds end, I charge thee on my blessing,
And husband you must go too.

ROBERTO
No, no not I.
I thank you Ursula, i'le not have my foot
Nor hand in any treason.

URSULA
Is it so much to kneel? you shall say nothing.
Unlesse you please, leave all the talk to me,

ROBERTO
I wo'not go, though the Duke send for me.

URSULA
How? that's a piece a treason.

ROBERTO
So, if I go not,
Shee'l betray me too; well Giovanni shall go too,
Where is he?

URSULA
Let me alone to conjure him.
Shall we go presently, delaies are dangerous.
The rascall George is gone too, all forsake me
In my distresse.

ROBERTO
What will you say Vrsula,
When you come there; what will the Dukes think on you?
Or who shall suffer for your impudence?
And what? that is considerable, I have
No mind to go agen.

URSULA
Then I'le spoile the Garden,
Break up the hedges, and deface the works
Your darling Giovanni made; i'le let in
A regiment of swine, and all their Officers
To undermine the Castle he made last,
And fortified with Cannon, though I dye for't.

ROBERTO
More treason, well I will go, but I hope
You wo'not trudge this evening, if we must
Resolve upon't, let us do things discreetly.

URSULA
That was well said, nay, I am for discretion
For all my hast.

ROBERTO
I think it most convenient
To wait his businesse, coming forth his Chamber
To morrow morning Vrsula, and then let
Good natures work, to nights no time,
We must consult our Pillowes; what to say;
And how to place our words.

URSULA
Now 'tis my best
Pigeon, let's home instantly.

ROBERTO
A sober pace goes far, not too fast Vrsula,
Remembring the Proverb, and what followes;
We should march slow to save me from the gallows.

[Exit.

SCENE II

A Room in Cornari's House.

[Enter **FLORELLI** followed by **CORNARI** with a Pistol.

CORNARI
You have had your time of pleasure, can you pray?

FLORELLI
Pray, what do you mean Signior.

CORNARI
The Lady whom you have enjoy'd, commanded
I should present one of these two, or both
In token of her gratitude.

FLORELLI
This cannot
Be earnest sir.

CORNARI
These are the Jewells
Which you must wear sir next your heart: how de'e
Affect the lustre of this toy? 'tis bright,
But here's a thing will sparkle.

FLORELLI
I am lost.
Is this the promise of my safety?

CORNARI
Yes,
This will secure all, thou dull Ilander,
'Cause you can dance, and vault upon a hobbihorse,
De'e think to mount Madonas here, and not
Pay for the sweet Carreere. Fool, to thy prayers,
For when these messengers salute thy heart,
Thy soul shall find, I'm an Italian,
And wo'not trust a life to him, whose tongue
Commands my honor.

FLORELLI
Art a Christian?

CORNARI
As much as comes to a Venetians faith,
That believes no man is moreto fit die
Then he, that has been capering with my wife.

FLORELLI

Ye cannot fir forget I was betrai'd,
Awake thy conscience, and let that answer
I have obey'd a dire necessity,
And was brought hither by a stratagem.

CORNARI
'Tis all one Signior; I presume you gave
Consent to the deere matter of delight,
Which is not held convenient you should talk of.

[Presents a pistol at him.

FLORELLI
Hold.

CORNARI
Hope not to breath ten minutes, gather up
Those thoughts you would have wait upon you to
Another world.

FLORELLI
Then 'tis high time to think
Of other matters, though you have cruelly
Resolv'd there is no safety for your fame,
To let me still be numbred with the living.
(Which if your scattered reason were collected,
I could refute,) but I'le not hope it now,)
Since most ignobly 'gainst the rules of honor,
And faith already forfeit, you will make
This undefenced pile your sacrifice,
Yet do not kill me twice.

CORNARI
Twice?

FLORELLI
Such a rage
Were infinite; practise not cruelty
Upon my second life, by murdering my
Eternity, allow to my last breath,
Leave to discharge the weight of many sinnes
Into the bosome of some confessor.

CORNARI
This may be granted, 'tis not much unreasonable.

FLORELLI
Your charity will think it fit to allow

Some minutes to collect my self.

CORNARI
To shew
My design has no malice in't, i'le do
Your soul that office, though our bodies must not
Enjoy this aire together many howrs.
I'le send one to you.

[Exit.

FLORELLI
The innocence of a Saint,
Wod not secure his life from an Italian
When his revenge is fixt. In what black hour
Did I salute the world, that I am thrown
Upon so hard a fate? it is not fit
To expostulate with heaven, or I could say
Something in my defence, (as I am man)
To keep this mighty rock from falling on me,
My tutelar Angell be at counsell with
My thoughts, and if there be a path of safety
Direct my trembling steps to find, and tast it.

[Enter **CORNARI** in a Friers habit.

Has kept his word, and 'tis no time to trifle,
As y'are a Priest, and by that sacred order
And scapular you wear, not onely hear me
But use your pious art to save from ruine
A man condemn'd for that which heaven and you
Call vertue, for not doing a black deed
Would damn three soules at once, & if your power
Cannot prevail for mercy to my life,
I challenge you when I am dead, to be
A witnesse of my innocence.

CORNARI
This has
No shape of a confession.

FLORELLI
Nor do I
Under that holy seal discourse a story,
Yet Father I must throw my self upon
Your Charity. Know therefore I am betraid,
And by the plot of him that owes this Palace
(Whose name is never like to meet my knowledge)

Snatch'd up, one fatall evening, and forc'd hither
By some dark ministers he had employ'd
(I know not which way) to this fatall chamber.
I shudder but to name what impious act
Against his own, and his dear Ladies honor
He had design'd for me; Her chaster soul
Should have been stain'd, in his distrust of heaven,
To blesse him with an heir, and her white treasure,
By me a stranger rifled, had not providence.
Chain'd up our blood, so that the hours he gave
To serve his black ambition, and our lust,
We onely spent in prayers for his conversion.

CORNARI
Ha!

FLORELLI
This yet he knowes not, and it is not safe
To appear in our own vertue, since the justice
We did our peace, in crossing his expectance
May improve his rage to both our ruines. This
Sad story frights you, there is horror in't,
But 'tis an hour, the last, without some miracle
To rescue me (a man disarm'd) from violence,
Nor dare I mock heaven now, or hang upon
My soul the burden of a lie, when tis
Taking her last eternall flight, It is not
A fear to dye afflicts me, with my faith
And innocence about me; I have look'd
Death in the face, and be it thought no boast
To say, I have taught others by example
To march up to the ugliest face of danger.
But to die thus dishonorably, to be
Sent out o'th world i'th dark, without a name
Or any account to those, to whom I owe
My blood, and birth? persons that carry names
Of honor in my Country? This doth stagger me
To quit my life, and may excuse my addresse
To you, who have Authority from heaven
To take his fury off, whom otherwise
I expect my violent executioner.
I have some tremblings for his Lady, whose
Most holy tears, stream'd through my soul compassion,
And charm'd my blood, tears, if he durst have patience
Were powerfull enough to beg from heaven
That blessing which he fondly thinks to hasten▪
With losse of his eternity.

CORNARI
No more.

[Exit **CORNARI** hastily, having thrown off the habit. Enter again with **CLAUDIANA**.

Forgive me, oh forgive me Claudiana,
And if my sin of forcing thy obedience
Beyond the rules of honor, and of marriage
Have not quite murd'red thy affection;
Wish me a little life for my repentance.

CLAUDIANA
I joy to hear this from you.

FLORELLI
There's work within me, and so deep a seuse
Of my own shame and sorrow, that I feel
My heart already weeping out a bath
To make thee white agen.

CLAUDIANA
Sir, in what best
I understand, I must ask you forgivenesse.

CORNARI
Ha! mine, for what, betraying thee to darkness?

CLAUDIANA
For disobeying your command.

CORNARI
Thou didst
The impious act by my design, which takes
Thy guilt away, and spreads the leprosie
Upon my self.

CLAUDIANA
Although you kill me sir,
I must remove the cloud, and let you see
Me as I am, not chang'd from my first innocence.

CORNARI
Possible?

CLAUDIANA
Most easie, where there is
A chast resolve, and I must tell you sir,
Although I wanted courage to oppose

Your passion, when your reason, and religion
Were under violence of your will, my heart
Resolv'd to try my own defence, and rather
Then yeeld my self a shamefull spoile to lust,
By my own death to quit my name from scandall;
But providence determin'd better for me,
And made me worth a strangers piety,
Whom your chice meant the ruine of my honor;
If this want entertainment in your faith,
'Tis peace to my poor heart that I have many
White witnesses in Heaven.

CORNARI [Coming forward]
You have done no feats then?
My wife is chast.

FLORELLI
I cannot sir engage
My last breath to a nobler truth.

CORNARI
'Tis so—
You may withdraw Claudiana;

[Exit **CLAUDIANA**.

By what
Has been exprest, though I am satisfied,
You are not guilty in the fact, as I
Expected, 'tis not safe, when I consider
My own fame in the story, that you live sir.
I must not trust you longer with a secret
That by my tamenesse may hereafter spread
The infamy abroad: there's no avoiding—

[Shows a pistol.

FLORELLI
Then I must die?

CORNARI
Perhaps you have some hope
This engine may deceive me, and my fortune
Not coming better arm'd, give you the advantage
To use your strength, upon my single person!
I know you are active, but i'le make sure work.

[Exit.

FLORELLI
Till now I did not reach the precipice.
My heart would mutinie, but my hands are naked,
And can do nothing.

[Enter **CORNARI** with **BRAVOS** arm'd.

A knot of murderers! arme me with a sword,
And let me die fighting against you all.
I'le say y'are noble hangmen, and not throw
One curse among you.

CORNARI
I've one word to say sir.
Let none approach,
The fatall doom I threatned is revers'd;
Throw off your wonder, and believe you may
Live long, if not in Venice, and your safety
Is more confirm'd at Distance, you are noble,
An honor to your nation. Here is gold,
I know not how you may be furnished sir
For travell hence, bills of exchange may fail.
These will defray a present charge; betray
No wonder, take it.

[Gives him money.

FLORELLI
I'le accept your bounty,
And will not ask to whom I owe all this,
Forgive me that. I thought you not so honorable.
So when you please, i'le take my leave.

CORNARI
Not yet.
By such attendants ss you came to me,
I have provided sir for your departure.
Your duties gentlemen. You know my purpose.

[The **BRAVOS** blind him, and bind him as before. Exeunt.

[Enter **CLAUDIANA**.

CORNARI
Resume thy place within my soul Claudiana,
When I have done my sorrow for what's past
Weel smile, and kisse for ever.

[Exeunt.

[Enter a **SERVANT** with a letter.

SERVANT
A letter sir.

CORNARI
From whence?

SERVANT
Your Nephew now a Prisoner.

CORNARI
Let him rot, and give 'em back the paperkite.

SERVANT
The messenger is gone.

CORNARI
Then he expects no answer.

[**CORNARI** ready]

CLAUDIANA
You may read it.

CORNARI [Reads]
Sir, I send not to you for reliefe, nor to
Mediate my pardon. I have not liv'd after
The rate to deserve your bread to feed me,
Nor your breath to save me. I onely beg
That you would put me into your prayers,
And forgivenesse, and believe, I do not wish life,
But to redeem my self from past impieties,
And satisfie by a repentance the dishonors
Have beene done to you, by the worst of men. Malipiero.
This is not his usual stile.

CLAUDIANA
This miracle may be.

CORNARI
I do want faith.

CLAUDIANA
And sent a blessing to reward our penitence.

Heaven has a spacious charity.

CORNARI
Thou art all goodnesse.

[Exit.

SCENE III

A Street

[Enter the **BRAVOS**, they lay **FLORELLI** down and Exeunt. **FLORELLI** recovers.

FLORELLI
Sure this is gold!

[Enter **3 GENTLEMEN.**

OMNES
Florelli.

FLORELLI
The same.

1ST GENTLEMAN
Thy looks are wild.

2ND GENTLEMAN
Where in the name of wonder hast thou been?

FLORELLI
I am drop'd from the Moon.

3RD GENTLEMAN
The Moon.

FLORELLI
I was snatch'd up in a whirlwind,
And din'd and sup'd at Cynthia's own table,
Where I drank all your healths in Nectar gentlemen,
Do yee want money? if you have a mind
To return viceroyes, let's take shipping instantly.

1ST GENTLEMAN
And whither then?

FLORELLI
For new discoveries,
A cloud will take us up at Sea.

2ND GENTLEMAN
'Tis morning.

FLORELLI
To drink, and then aboord, no matter whither
I'le keep this for a monument.

3RD GENTLEMAN
That bag?

FLORELLI
Do not profane it, 'twas Endimions pillow
Stuffd with horne shavings of the Moon, it had
The vertue when she clap'd it ore my head
To bring me thence invisible through the air;
The moon does mobble up her self sometime in't.
Where she will shew a quarter face, and was
The first that wore a black bag.

1ST GENTLEMAN
But dost hear?

FLORELLI
No inquisitions if you will leave Venice.
Let's drink and spoon away with the next vessell.
A hundred leagues hence, I may tell you wonders.
Here is a chime to make Ring Oberon,

[Shows the gold.

Queen Mab, and all her fayries turn o'th toe boyes.

2ND GENTLEMAN
He's mad I think.

[Exeunt.

SCENE IV

An Apartment in the Duke's Palace.

[Enter **URSULA, ROBERTO, GIOVANNI**.

URSULA
I could not sleep all this night for dreaming,
O'my poor suckling.

ROBERTO
peace I say and wait
In silence Ursula.

GIOVANNI
You may excuse me yet.
I wo'd not see his excellence.

URSULA
'Tis not my meaning boy, thou shouldst appear
Unless there be necessity, you may stay, ith'e next Chamber.

[Exit **GIOVANNI**.

[Enter a **COURTIER**.

URSULA
I beseech you Signior, is this grace coming forth.

CORNARI
Not yet.

URSULA
I have an humble sute, I must deliver
A paper to his graces own hand,
I hope his grace can read.

[Exit **COURTIER**.

ROBERTO
Why how now bagpiper.

URSULA
Nay, theres no harm in't what if he can,
You will be talking, did not I say
I would speak all my self.

ROBERTO
But Ursula what do you think now will become onus
When you have told your tale, though I am innbcent.
It will be no great credit, nor much comfort
To see you whipt my Ursula, I would
Be sorry for my part to peep through a Pillory

And have an even reckoning with my ears,
Having no more hair to keep warm, and hide
The poor concavities.

URSULA
Never fear it husband.

ROBERTO
I will so curse you Ursula, and once
A day, bind your body to a pear tree,
And thrash your hanches till you stink agen;
For ought I know thou hast committed treason,
Look to't, and bring me off with all my quarters
If I be maim'd or cropt, I'le flea thee Vrsula,
And stuffe thy skin with straw, and hang thee up
To keep the fruit from Crowes, and after burn it.
To kill the Caterpillars, come, be wise in time,
And let Thomazo quietly be hang'd,
Or headed yet, and talk no more, he is
But one, and has a young neck to endure it.
We are old, and sha'not shew with half the grace
Without our heads, 'twill be a goodly sight
To see our faces grin upon two poles,
To tell the gaping world how we came thither
To perch, and stink in unity, be wise,
And leave Thomazo to the Law.

URSULA
Can you be so uncharitable, oh Tyrant!

[Enter **DUKE, MARINO**.

May it please your excellence, my husband and
My self.

ROBERTO
She has put me in already.

URSULA
Humbly beseech a pardon for our son.

DUKE
Your son Giovanni, where is he?

URSULA
He waites in the next Chamber.

DUKE

Call him in.

[Exit **URSULA**.

What is the fact?
It must be an offence next treason, if we
Deny him pardon.

ROBERTO [aside]
I fear 'tis much about the matter.

DUKE
What is the fact?

[Enter **URSULA** and **GIOVANNI**; they kneel.

URSULA
We do beseech you grant a pardon first,
And then you shall know all.

DUKE
That were preposterous justice.
Why dost thou kneel Giovanni?

GIOVANNI
To beg your mercy sir
To him, for whom my mother kneeles

DUKE
She askes thy pardon.

GIOVANNI
Mine? Let me offend first.

DUKE
He's innocent.

URSULA
No matter what he saies, my husband knowes it.

ROBERTO [aside]
She']l make sure of me.

URSULA
And if your highness will but grant the pardon,
Your grace shall not repent, but thank me for
The best discovery; i'le not bribe your excellence,
But I will give you for it, what you'l hold

As pretious as your Dukedome.

DUKE
The old woman
Raves, you had best send her to the house
Of the insanity.

ROBERTO [aside]
So! she's to be whip'd already.

DUKE
What do you say Roberto!

ROBERTO
I say nothing,
But that I think my wife will hardly mend upon't.

DUKE
Upon what?

ROBERTO
On whipping, if it like your highnesse,
She cannot feel those small corrections.
I have taw'd hunting Poles, and hemp upon her,
And yet could do no good.

URSULA
Let not your grace mind him, give me a pardon,
And if I do not make good all my promise,
You shall hang my husband, and flea me alive.

DUKE
What's that paper?

ROBERTO
Ge't him, thou shouldst have done this afore.

[She gives a paper to the **DUKE**.

I am prepar'd, more bone and flesh upon me
If the businesse come to hanging, were a curtesie.

URSULA
Nay 'tis there in black and white, you'l find it
Giovanni is your son, that was the Gardiner,
And he that is in prison poor Thomazo
My lawfully begotten.

DUKE
Chang'd in their infancie.

URSULA
And since conceal'd out of ambition
To see my own a great man.

ROBERTO [aside]
I feel the knot under my ear.

URSULA
I durst not trust my husband.

ROBERTO [aside]
That was not much amisse.

URSULA
He has not wit enough to keep my secrets.

ROBERTO [aside]
Oh what a blessing has that man whose wife
Knowes when to hold her peace!

MARINO
Sir, if we may compare their tracts of life,
I shall believe your noblenesse liv'd there
In Giovanni, not supprest in poverty,
And their rude course condition, notwithstanding
The helpes of Education, which seldome
Do correct nature in Thomazo's low
And abject spirit.

DUKE
I'me too full, I must
Disperse my swelling joyes or be dissolv'd,
Summon our friends, invite Bellaura hither.

[Exit **MARINO**.

Art thou my son?

GIOVANNI
I would I were so blest.
Iow'd you duty sir before, and now
My knees encline with double force to humble
The doubtfull Giovanni.

DUKE

Let that name
Be lost, take all my blessings in Thomazo.

URSULA
What think you of this Roberto.

ROBERTO
Why? I think
The Duke is mad, and when he finds his wits
Hee'l hang us both yet.

DUKE
Now I find the reason.
And secret of my nature: but tell me
What after so long silence, made you now
Open the cloud that had conceal'd my son?

ROBERTO
I know not sir—now Ursula.

URSULA
The weaknesse of a woman, and a mother
That would be loath to see her naturall child
Dye like a bird upon a bough for treason,
Nature will work, a mother is a mother,
And your son, by the opening of this riddle
Restor'd, I hope all shall be well agen.

ROBERTO
Would I were fair wash'd, yet out of my pickle.

URSULA
What think you now?

ROBERTO
I wish, I wish I could not think.

[Enter **SENATORS** and **CORNARI**.

CORNARI
We hear of wonders sir.

DUKE
This is my son.

CORNARI
With our most glad embraces let us hold you.

GIOVANNI
Ever a servant to your gravities.

ROBERTO
The skie clears up.

[Enter **BELLAURA, MARINO**.

DUKE
Bellaura, now receive not Giovanni,
But Contarini's son my deer Thomazo.

BELLAURA
My heart hath wings to meet him.

THOMAZO
Oh my happinesse!

DUKE
Pause a little.

ROBERTO
I melt agen Vrsula, the Duke points at us,
And carries fireworks in his eyes,

DUKE
Though we did grant a pardon for your son,
You are subject to the censure of our lawes
For this imposture.

ROBERTO
I knew't would come, now telltale, will you beg
The favour we may hang till we be dead?
Sweet Giovanni Thomazo speak for us,
Not guilty my Lord, I am not guilty,
Spare me, and let my wife be burn'd or hang'd,
Or drown'd, or any thing you shall think fit,
You shall find me reasonable,
Who shall beg our pardon?

URSULA
Mercy oh mercy.

THOMAZO
Let me beseech you for their pardon sir.
They alwaies us'd me civilly.

BELLAURA

Let me joine.

SENATOR
And all of us, this is a day of triumph.

DUKE
It shall be so.

ROBERTO
A Jubile, a Jubile, here comes Thomazo,
I shall speak treason presently.

URSULA
Now heaven preserve your sweet graces.

[Enter **THOMAZO, MALIPIERO**.

GIOVANNI
Mercy, oh mercy, my indulgent father.

URSULA
Art thou come boy?

GIOVANNI
Boy? stand away good woman.

URSULA
I have procur'd thy pardon, mary have I child.

GIOVANNI
I wo'd 'twere true, thou wert ever a loving Crone.

ROBERTO
You may believe her son.

GIOVANNI
Son, the old fellow's mad.

URSULA
I say thou art pardon'd,
You must kneel to me now, and this good
Old man, and ask us blessing.

MARINO
Your name is prov'd Giovanni now, the Duke
Has found another son.

GIOVANNI

What shall become of me?

DUKE
You shall be onely punish'd to return,
And dig as he hath done, and change your name
To Giovanni, nature was not willing
You should forget your trade, where's my Thomazo?

GIOVANNI
Are you my father?

ROBERTO
So my wife assures me.

GIOVANNI
Are you my mother?

URSULA
I my deere child.

GIOVANNI
And you Signior Thomazo, that was I?

THOMAZO
And you Giovanni with the inside outward

GIOVANNI
And must I be a Gardiner? I am glad on't.
Pray give me a couple of blessings, and a spade,
And fico for this frippery. I'le thank
My destiny that has yet kept my thread
To a better use then hanging.

CORNARI.
Let nothing
Of punishment profane this day, I must
Implore your mercy upon this young man,

[Pointing to **MALIPIERO**.

Whose future life may recompence his past
Impieties, and make him serviceable
To honor and good men.

DUKE
You shew a charity,
If I have heard a truth in some sad stories,
Hee's yours and pardon'd.

MARINO
Y'are a miracle
Of goodnesse, 'tis too much to look upon,
Whom I have with such impudence offended.
Command me sir abroad until by some
Years well employ'd, a pennance for my crimes
I may be thought one worthy to be own'd
Your Kinsman.

DUKE
Agen, welcome my Thomazo,
My dearest pledge, till now I was no father;
In him, the want of hope my thoughts opprest,
In thee my fortunes, and my name are blest.

[Exeunt.

JAMES SHIRLEY – A CONCISE BIBLIOGRAPHY

The following includes years of first publication, and of performance if known, together with dates of licensing by the Master of the Revels if available.

TRAGEDIES
The Maid's Revenge (licensed 9th February 1626; printed, 1639)
The Traitor (licensed 4th May 1631; printed, 1635)
Love's Cruelty (licensed 14th November 1631; printed, 1640)
The Politician (acted, 1639; printed, 1655)
The Cardinal (licensed 25th May 1641; printed, 1652).

TRAGI-COMEDIES
The Grateful Servant (licensed 3rd November 1629 as The Faithful Servant; printed 1630)
The Young Admiral (licensed 3rd July 1633; printed 1637)
The Coronation (licensed 6th February 1635, as Shirley's, but printed in 1640 as a work of John Fletcher)
The Duke's Mistress (licensed 18th January 1636; printed 1638)
The Gentleman of Venice (licensed 30th October 1639; printed 1655)
The Doubtful Heir (printed 1652), licensed as Rosania, or Love's Victory in 1640
The Imposture (licensed 10th November 1640; printed 1652)
The Court Secret (printed 1653).

COMEDIES
Love Tricks, or the School of Complement (licensed 10th February 1625; printed under its subtitle, 1631)
The Wedding (ca. 1626; printed 1629)
The Brothers (licensed 4th November 1626; printed 1652)
The Witty Fair One (licensed 3rd October 1628; printed 1633)
The Humorous Courtier (licensed 17th May 1631; printed 1640).

The Changes, or Love in a Maze (licensed 10th January 1632; printed 1639)
Hyde Park (licensed 20th April 1632; printed 1637)
The Ball (licensed 16th November 1632; printed 1639)
The Bird in a Cage, or The Beauties (licensed 21st January 1633; printed 1633)
The Gamester (licensed 11th November 1633; printed 1637)
The Example (licensed 24th June 1634; printed 1637)
The Opportunity (licensed 29th November 1634; printed 1640)
The Lady of Pleasure (licensed 15th October 1635; printed 1637)
The Royal Master (acted and printed 1638)
The Constant Maid, or Love Will Find Out the Way (printed 1640)
The Sisters (licensed 26th April 1642; printed 1653).
Honoria and Mammon (printed 1659)

DRAMAS
A Contention for Honor and Riches (printed 1633), morality play
The Triumph of Peace (licensed 3rd February 1634; printed 1634), masque
The Arcadia (printed 1640), pastoral tragicomedy
St. Patrick for Ireland (printed 1640), neo-miracle play
The Triumph of Beauty (ca. 1640; printed 1646), masque
The Contention of Ajax and Ulysses (printed 1659), entertainment
Cupid and Death (performed 26th March 1653; printed 1659), masque

www.ingramcontent.com/pod-product-compliance
Lightning Source LLC
Chambersburg PA
CBHW060623070426
42448CB00046B/2008